My Pretentious Memoir

MY PRETENTIOUS MEMOIR

PART DEUX

DONALD J. HURZELER

Kua Bay Publishing LLC

First Edition

Print ISBN   978-0-9981063-8-0

eBook ISBN   978-0-9981063-9-7

DEDICATION

I met my wife, Linda, in 1967. I had a broken foot, smashed the night before in a car accident I will tell you about later. I was just transferring into Chapman University from Pierce Junior College, where I had studied advanced physics, non-mathematical calculus, Greek, Latin and the classics, or something like that, while trying to get my grades high enough to get into a real college. Linda was an incoming freshman. She was the single best-looking incoming freshman in the history of universities anywhere. I fell in love with her the moment I saw her. On our first date I told her I loved her and that we would be married. We were and we still are, some 53 years later.

If I had any class at all, I would give her co-authoring credit for this book. She was often the one who remembered the stories. She is always the one to hear them on the first read, hot off the printer. She is the one who saves me from myself and says useful things like, "Is there another word you can substitute for 'fuck' in that sentence?"

Well, I have no class, so this book is mine and mine alone. And, after reading the first draft, Linda said she was just as happy not being that closely tied to its content...so win/win.

Linda Levy Collins Hurzeler is the love of my life, has been for over half a century, will be forever. As far as I am concerned, she is responsible for much of whatever success I have had, she played a significant role in producing two great children with me, and she lights up my life every single day. I love Linda...have from minute one, and I dedicate this book to her.

TABLE OF CONTENTS

CHAPTER ONE

The Explainer About What This Book Is All About

You do not have to read my last book, *What's Left of Don,* to read this book. It would be helpful if you did read that book, as it would make me more money; however, it is not required. This book stands on its own. A book of life stories, memories, adventures, oddities, true events, minor exaggerations and one outright lie...all from my fairly long life, thus far.

During my corporate life of some 40-plus years, I had the persona of someone who was reliable, a good teammate, honest, energetic, straightforward, a good communicator and leader, as well as a person who was inclusive and caring.... with a quirky sense of humor. All of that was pretty much true. However, there was a personal side that the people at work rarely saw...my quite flawed human side. That side led me to places both embarrassing and fun...with an emphasis on "embarrassing." These were the "I'm not very proud of that" moments. A lot of them are going to make you laugh out loud. A few are not.

Over the years I have heard, "Oh, I wish I could be just like you." I hear it even more now that I am retired, living in Hawaii and very active on social media, like Facebook. Well, I like me and I am happy to be me, but be careful what you wish for. Read these stories and then tell me how you feel about your life. I am guessing you will have renewed appreciation for your own good sense.

And I don't really get into my big time battle with the cancer that nearly got me, the ups and downs we all have in our lives, or the "not quite as much fun as I expected" aspects of aging that are now finding their way into my daily life. But out of all that I hope one thing does become clear...we can survive our mistakes... you and I...and enjoy the life that WE have...because it might just actually be WAY better than that shiny superstar life you see on TV or on Facebook or watching someone standing on a stage running for election. I'm guessing if those people wrote a book this honest about their lives...our hair might catch fire.

CHAPTER TWO

Raised Like A Free-Range Chicken

Right off the bat, I would like to blame most of my eccentricities in life on my grand dad, Ed Hurzeler, and my dad, Jim Hurzeler. They taught me "freedom" before I even knew the word. I like to say that I was raised as a "free-range" kid, and I was. Let me share just a taste of that before I launch into the results of my upbringing.

My dad thought I was too skinny as a child, which I was. I was athletic, but, man, I was skinny. Net result, my normal-sized ears stuck out like barn doors and you could see the outline of my ribs through my tee shirts. Dad took action.

I must have been eight or nine when I started getting a glass of beer at dinner to "increase my appetite"...according to Dad...who was not exactly a doctor or a nutritional expert. It was just a normal drink to me. I loved it. I cannot ever recall it giving me a buzz...as a kid. I do recall it used to horrify our relatives when they came over for dinner and I was having a beer. But my folks were country folks and they did a number of things that horrified our more refined relatives and friends.

As I got into maybe seventh grade, my mom came up with an even better idea to fatten me up...daily homemade chocolate chip malts with half-and-half and crème de menthe. Holy shit were they good! I could hardly wait to get home to have a big blender's worth. Did kind of whet my appetite for the beer that would be coming my way at dinner. Stoked.

And my folks never really did keep track of me. I was semi-reliable and they had their hands full with jobs and my sister, so I was kind of on my own. That resulted in my trying things early that most people might not experience until later on in life, and all of that ended up giving me courage...maybe too much courage...

3

and confidence. I never worried about failing at anything because failure and success were treated much the same at my house...either not noticed at all or only lightly mentioned.

Although we lived in a fancy neighborhood growing up, Palos Verdes Estates, California, my folks never lost their ties to country life...having been raised in Wyoming, Oklahoma and Colorado. They wanted to make sure I got to experience and appreciate that life, so every summer we drove off to Colorado to visit relatives. Then my dad had this great idea, let's send 12-year-old Donny...that is me...to visit the grandfolks in Colorado...with transportation provided by that elite carrier, Greyhound Bus Lines.

My grandparents on my dad's side were simple country folks...whom I loved with all my heart. They lived outside of Boulder, Colorado, in the then completely rural area of Niwot. Their ranch was simple, but the stuff of a kid's dreams. They had turkeys and chickens and grew hay. My aunt and her family lived in a big house (big family) just across the pasture. There were cottonwood trees, a screen door that had a sound when it slammed shut that I can still hear, and the Axelson boys lived nearby. I loved going to see Mom and Dad Hurzeler.

When I say they were simple country folks, I do not mean stupid. They were smart in ways I was not. They did not follow all the rules I had been brought up on. What guided decisions was the question, "What needs to be done?"

So, at the age of 12, I took the bus trip from California to Boulder to go spend a couple of weeks on my grandparents' ranch. Traveled by myself. Met my first prostitute at the bus station at midnight in Gallup, New Mexico...but did not engage her services or even really understand what her services might have been. Arrived in Colorado with no plan and no idea what to expect for my upcoming stay.

I was getting to see that things were quite different on the farm, so, as has always been my way, I decided to test the limits. "Granddad, do you have a gun I can borrow? I want to go rabbit hunting." No problem. Granddad comes back with a loaded rifle and gives it to me. He advises me against aiming it toward the house or at any of the neighbor's cows. Gives me two pockets of bullets to go with it. No supervision. No gun safety class. No "let's go plink a few cans so you can get a feel of the weapon." Instead...here is your gun; have fun killing stuff.

Well, that worked out and no rabbits were hurt in the adventure. Any number of cow plops were destroyed, me pretending they were rabbits.

Next up...let's see what I can do to get me a little freedom. We were way out in the country. Even the Axelson boys were quite a distance away. I had no bike and all the roads were dirt. So, let's ask Grandpa if I can borrow his red Dodge pickup truck. I asked. He didn't say a word...just tossed me the keys. Did I mention I was 12? He didn't even ask me where I was going....which was a good thing, because I had no idea.

I was off...kind of. Took me a while to figure out the stick shift. I had learned to drive back home on a stick shift, but this one was different. Took a while, but I got it figured out...and off I went.

The first thing I learned was that dirt roads were not the same as paved roads... not even close. The area near the ranch was pretty flat and the roads were pretty good, but still it was dirt that was loose in some places, had some ruts that you might not see until it was too late and there was this thing alongside the road that I had never dealt with at home...a ditch. More about the ditch coming right up.

Not having any idea which way town was, I just drove. I soon found out that dirt could be both fun and dangerous...a combination I have loved my entire life. The fun was due to the fact that you could drift or slide your vehicle on dirt quite easily. If you did it on purpose, it was fun. If it happened, as my son used to say, "on accident," it was dangerous. In fact, that is how I learned about the ditch.

I was busy speeding down long empty dirt roads in "my" red Dodge pickup, really out in the middle of pretty much vacant farmland, bothering no one other than the occasional chicken that had to hurry to get out of my way. It was very flat in that area, so even though there were no road signs and I did not know the area, I could easily keep my eyes on the trees around my grandparents' house, making it possible for me to navigate back there eventually. I guess they could have followed my progress by just following the cloud of dirt I was creating as I sped along.

The driving settled into a great game. I would get the pickup up to just the right speed, head into a turn and tap the brakes as I entered it. I would then start to slide and would use the steering wheel to try to guide the drifting truck around the turn...which turned out to not be foolproof...with me as the fool.

I got good at this drifting thing quickly. I got so good that I could almost get the truck sideways as I drifted around the turn. Should mention it was so flat I could see well ahead, even around the turn, so I was in no danger of running into another car or cow or whatever.

And then I met a new obstacle. I hit a turn hard, but it was not like the other turns. This turn featured ruts in the road and something I learned later was called "a washboard"...an area of many small ruts in a pattern possibly resulting from the last time they graded the road...an area that sent massive vibrations through the suspension of the Dodge. Turns out that ruts and washboard and loose dirt add up to no traction. Much as I turned that steering wheel, nothing happened. Oh, I was drifting, but there was no turning in the drift...I kept going straight. That is when I found out about the ditch.

Country roads in that area had ditches alongside them for drainage and maybe even to help with irrigation on the various farms...not sure, I am not a farm expert. The ditch was not deep, and it was dry when I hit it. But the impact was jarring because I hit it at quite a high speed; the airbag failed to go off since it would be 40 more years before airbags were invented. The seat belt failed to hold me since it would be 10 more years before they were invented...and 20 more before I actually started using them (I am not an early adopter of anything that might hold me down). I was flung across the vehicle and nearly knocked out. The pickup ended up half on its side, wheels still spinning despite my foot not being on the gas, and covered in a swirling cloud of dirt. One back tire was in the ditch and the ditch, while dry, was both muddy and grassy on the bottom, so the wheel kept on spinning without getting any traction.

I was able to pull myself across the vehicle and shut it off. I was uninjured and aware of my situation, so that was good. The vehicle did not look to be a total wreck, also good news. I now had to find a way to get out to survey the damage. I crawled out the driver's side window because it was closest to the ground...quite close in fact.

I'm sure this was wishful thinking then and revisionist history now, but the pickup appeared to be unharmed...maybe a couple of small dents and a scratch or two, but...other than the liberal covering of dirt and mud, undamaged. It was, however, nearly on its side and stuck in a muddy ditch. I did not even try to get it out...it was in there.

I was a long way from the ranch, and I was not eager to return home without the pickup. So, I sat there. I sat there for probably an hour...no one drove by. When someone did come by, they helped me tip the pickup back on its tires, got a rope out of the back, tied the rope to their hay truck and "my" pickup and pulled that sucker out of the ditch. We both looked it over carefully, agreed it was in drivable condition and that was that. I thanked him over and over. He never once asked why I would be driving Ed Hurzeler's pickup into a ditch, with me obviously being 12 years old. I am pretty sure he never mentioned it to my granddad...at least I never got any questions about it. Country life...lots to be said for it.

I then waited for the sun to go down. I drove back home, got the well water going and a bucket of water and washed the pickup in the dark to remove as much of the evidence of the wreck as possible.

You might think that my granddad would look the pickup over to check for damage after I had it out for so many hours. Nope. Granddad had one eye. He once had a hay handling hook come loose on him and it had gone directly into his eye, so he did what country folks did back then, put some tape over his sunglasses to cover the eye...and that was that. Hey, he still had the one good eye, so no problem. But as a result, his eyesight was not keen, and he never bothered to look the truck over. That truck was still around and usable when he died...decades later...so I must not have done too much harm.

I learned a big lesson that day. Well, that is bullshit. I learned nothing, just another "if it doesn't kill you it was probably fun" moment from my youth.

CHAPTER THREE

Wrongs of Passage

I had an interesting run with cigarettes and alcohol. Never took any drugs of any kind...not even once...not even a puff of marijuana. But I did like my Marlboros and just about any kind of alcohol I could get my hands on. Cigarettes are 45 years behind me now. Have not had any alcohol in over 30 years and we should all be glad for that change in my life...as you will see.

I became a hell of a good athlete, but my athletic activities burned off every calorie I ever ingested in those days. I entered high school as a 118-pound freshman. I went from being a football star in grade school to a target for the bigger and older high school players, who just mowed me down. Net result, I hated football and decided to concentrate on track and field, which turned out to be an excellent choice and changed my life forever in a very positive way.

By the time I was through with my sophomore year, I was growing and filling out. I also learned that no one in the family seemed to care if I just grabbed a beer any damn time I wanted. So, I grabbed. It was not too long after that change in behavior that I learned that two or more beers could give you a hell of a buzz. Loved the buzz.

A buddy introduced me to cigarettes at 16 years of age and I liked those little guys right from the start. I had no money in those days, and that was about the only thing that limited my smoking. I smoked before school, during school and after school. I kept a carton of cigarettes in my locker at school, since my parents had found all my hollowed-out book hiding spots at home. (Handy hint to anyone wanting to hide something in a book...don't leave the book pages you cut out from the center of the book in the waste basket your parents will eventually dump when they can no longer stand your filthy room. They will find those pages, trace them back to your cut-up hideout book and bust you big time with whatever condoms, cigarettes or porno you may have hidden there.)

So, I was getting pretty good at track. The assistant vice principal of our high school loved athletics and, in fact, owned a minority interest in the Los Angeles Rams. He was a big scary guy and we all avoided him, if we could. I could not. He had taken on the task of keeping me eligible for track. This included intimidating teachers in classes where I was failing and generally keeping an eye on my behavior. I did not know about the teacher intimidation until years later when I finally learned how my D and F grades sometimes turned into C-minuses until the track season was over. So, thanks go to him for that excellent service and my apologies to any teacher who had to put up with that kind of bullying. Had I known anything about it then I would have....well, I would have thanked him. I needed to stay eligible. I had very little else going for me at that time.

I did not know that he was keeping an eye on me...literally. He apparently had a key to my locker and checked it from time to time to see what was there. What was there were my cigarettes. Not for long. Early one morning I rushed to my locker before first class and all of a sudden found myself about a foot off the ground pinned up against a wall being pushed repeatedly into that wall. Behind me, the assistant VP who had me in one hand and my carton of cigarettes in the other. He threatened to beat the hell out of me if he ever caught me with cigarettes again. He then let me down, walked off calmly and went on about his business. The kids around me were pretty shocked that an administrator would threaten to beat up a kid, but they too were scared of this guy. They did start laughing nervously and telling me that I was in big trouble and would probably be suspended. Wrong... nothing ever happened. That was a warning and I never brought a cigarette on campus again. I did have a spot under the athletic stands that I did not consider to be on campus and that is where I hid, and often smoked, my cigarettes.

CHAPTER FOUR

Party On...Followed by, the Party is Over

Moving along to my later years in high school...

Only one other person in the world knows this story about me, and given my current life and respect for all things on the land and in the ocean, I am in no way proud of what happened, but it was more than 55 years ago and I was maybe 16 at the time...so please forgive me...

A buddy of mine and I had a few beers one night in my hometown of Palos Verdes, California. Palos Verdes had an attraction called Marineland. Marineland was all about dolphin shows, pilot whale and orca shows, fish displays, seal acts and the like...stuff I absolutely hate today. Back then, got to say, I loved it...did not think about the animals...did not think about their captivity...thought it was all great stuff.

Many of my classmates worked at Marineland in the summer. I might add that Marineland was on the back side of Palos Verdes with almost nothing around it and it was pretty much abandoned at night after the restaurant closed. By abandoned, I mean no security. They locked it up and everyone went home.

A lot of us who lived in PV also knew there was a drainage pipe that passed under a road and a wall...a pipe large enough to crawl through...right into Marineland. So we did.

One night my buddy and I decided to go see Corky...one of the trained orcas and star of the show. They also had a couple of trained pilot whales, one of them named Bubbles. We had watched them many times in their shows...looked like lovely, gentle animals. I think you can see where this is going.

The whales were not out in their big tank, they were in much smaller enclosures at night. The size of the enclosure looked like it would cut down on the distance I could ride the orca, but also made it quite easy to get on him. All I had to do was throw my leg across his body and hold onto his massive dorsal fin...looked simple enough.

Turns out this killer whale did not much like having a stranger try to ride him in the middle of the night in his small enclosure. I doubt that I made it even half a length of the pool before Corky slammed me hard into the side of the enclosure. I was lucky as heck the blow did not knock me out, as I was able to pull myself out of the water before the orca could circle back on me.

My buddy decided that he would pass on his attempt to go for a ride and we ran for the drainage pipe exit. Our orca-riding days had come to an abrupt halt.

Fortunately, my track and school schedule and lack of funds kept me away from alcohol most of the time. It really did not cause me many problems, other than one I just mentioned. But there was an exception...

My buddies and I had a party every Friday night. We had a friend who was the delivery guy for the local liquor store. We would call in an order and...voila... whatever liquor we could afford would arrive in about half an hour, usually Red Mountain wine (costing about $1.50 for a huge jug) or cheap beer. We would put Johnny Mathis on the record player, turn down the lights and see what we could get away with our girlfriends...usually not much, despite the availability of the liquor. We loved Friday nights.

Only two bad things ever happened at those parties. The first was that one of my friends had a buddy from his old hometown come to visit, and he brought him to the party. Apparently, the guy was not used to alcohol and kind of went nuts. We tried to calm him down and we put on some coffee to see if we could sober him up. While waiting for the coffee to heat up and while my girlfriend and I were dancing to some slow tune, I was quite surprised to see our visitor completely naked and taking a dump in the middle of the living room rug. That is something that is hard to get out of your mind. I can still see that guy all squatty down taking a dump. He was never invited back.

The other thing was worse. One fine night that party was busted by the police and the school administrators. The mom of one of my best friends, the owner of the apartment, was arrested. The kids who were caught got in trouble at school. Me...not so much. By just plain good luck, I was at the Southern Section California Interscholastic Federation Track and Field Finals, where I came in third in the low hurdles.

The next Monday I got called into the track coach's office. I was the captain of the track team and the only person on that team who had qualified for the California State Championship meet. Coach sat me down and told me what had happened while he and I were at the track meet. He also told me that one of the kids at the party had ratted me out (probably under horrific torture by the screws at the police station) as someone who had attended those parties in the past. He then asked me a fateful question...had I ever attended any of those parties?

Now, you should know that Coach was another big scary guy. He was tall, no nonsense and he demanded our respect. He was no one you would ever want to go up against. And, we loved him and respected him and would never want to disappoint him.

I thought for a moment and said, "Coach, do you want the truth?" And then came the biggest surprise of my life. His answer: "Not necessarily."

So that was what he got, not necessarily the truth. He thanked me and dismissed me. The next weekend I came in fourth in the California State Track and Field Finals and that led to a whole bunch of scholarship offers. One of them took me to Chapman University where I ended up graduating, meeting and marrying my wife, and then getting my first real job...one that lasted for 28 years before I changed to another company. It was at Chapman where I made NCAA Division II All-American and was later added to the Chapman University Athletic Hall of Fame and where I met a group of teammates, buddies, coaches and professors who remain my friends to this day. So, kind of an important deal in my life.

I never asked Coach about that incident until quite late in his life. Here's how that happened. We were having breakfast one morning and he was telling me stories about some of my teachers. Most of the stories were about what fine people they were even outside of school and how much fun they were to be around...a side we rarely got to see as their students. I brought up the incident with the scary vice principal and Coach laughed until he almost cried. He told me that the two of them had planned that out together. He also told me that he knew I smoked and really did not care, since I ran short distance sprints, but that he did not want me to find the kind of trouble that would get me kicked off the team or embarrass my teammates. And that he had hoped the scare would get me to stop that stupid habit (it did not).

He then told me about another one of my teachers. This was a teacher who had contacted me after school and told me that I should not accept any of the scholarship offers that were coming my way because I was a horrible student and did not deserve a seat in a college classroom. He suggested I learn a trade. I thought Coach was going to tell me that this was a teacher that the vice principal had bullied to keep me eligible. He was not...he had told this same thing to several athletes from the football and track team. He apparently just did not like athletes.

This breakfast with Coach was probably when I was about 55 years old and by then CEO of a company. I had earned an Associates of Arts degree, a Bachelor of Arts degree, and two professional designations, as a Chartered Property Casualty Underwriter and as a Chartered Life Underwriter, had attended graduate school at Kellogg School of Management at Northwestern University and Harvard University, and had written my first book. I had the passing thought of sending one of my books to that long-ago teacher, but Coach told me that he had committed suicide. I was sorry to hear that news; I hate that anyone finds life unbearable. Although that teacher's recommendation to not attend college pissed me off at the time, it probably solidified my commitment to going to college and graduating. Other than that one bad interaction, I always kind of liked him and I am extremely sad that his life ended as it did.

So, on that surprising and sad note, I blurted out the question I had long wanted to ask my straight arrow, "follow the rules" Coach... "Why did you choose to let me lie my way out of a difficult situation?"

Coach smiled and thought for a moment. He said he had screwed up a few times as a kid and would have hated to have one bad moment erase the future that he got to live. In the end, he had seen me work too hard to have it all come to a crashing halt for a party that I did not attend, even though I had attended similar parties in the past. He also told me that he had been approached by the coach of Stanford University about a full scholarship for me and he did not want to see that taken away. He then apologized for putting me in a position where I could so easily choose the morally wrong answer that would let me get away with something that many of my friends ended up getting disciplined for doing.

At that, I teared up, got up and hugged that great big scary Coach and told him I loved him.

I never learned who ratted me out...wouldn't want to know. They did what they thought was the right thing to do for whatever reason, and I was just as guilty as any of them.

This whole episode came at the end of my senior year. I had gotten ill right about that time and by the next weekend was sick as a dog. I ran the State Finals in 100-degree Bakersfield, California, heat, while sporting a 102-degree temperature on my own, with a sore throat and a swollen and split lip. I felt like I was dying... except for the few minutes right before and during the preliminary and finals races, when I felt like Superman and ran my fastest times ever. I was unable to participate in most of the end of the school year festivities, lost 35 of my then 165 pounds and was unable to participate in the high and low hurdles in the track and field event that served as the national championship meet in those days...the Golden West Invitational. Maybe a little bit of a karma payback for being given a pass on some bad behavior. If so, it was a good one, because to this day I regret not having been able to run in that particular event.

CHAPTER FIVE

My Full Scholarship to Stanford University...
Gone, but not Forgotten

So...Stanford University. I came from a family where the only person who had ever graduated from college...or even gone to college...was my beloved Uncle Pat. World War II and deep poverty kept my otherwise smart parents away from college and involved in either fighting the war in Europe...my dad was in the Signal Corps and went in on D-Day plus one at Omaha Beach, or supporting our troops here at home...my mom worked in an office at Camp Roberts Army Base in San Luis Obispo, California, during the war. So, I had no guiding light about things scholastic.

I was a smart kid who could get by with passing grades without studying, not really knowing that a grade of C was not really what was needed. I scored well on tests like the SAT...really well...but followed that up with a 2.0 overall grade point average. Which leads me to my Stanford story.

I knew nothing about Stanford University...nothing, other than the fact that their track coach was the coach of the U.S. Olympic team. I had been around him some, watched him on TV, read about him...Coach Payton Jordan was a hero of mine.

Coach Jordan knew nothing about me, except I was co-captain of my undefeated track team, had been a star athlete for a coach whom he admired and was on an improvement path that could take me right to the top. He needed another sprinter/hurdler and he set his sights on me.

I visited Coach Jordan on the Stanford campus. He worked me out and I did really well. He then took me to dinner, where he asked me about my grades. I told him that I had scored near the top on the SAT. He said that was great, but what about my grades? I told him that they were well above average. He wanted to know how much above average. I told him about ten percent. Now he was confused. He asked me to be specific...what did I consider to be "average"? I said that I was told a C was average, so a 2.0 would be average and I was at about a 2.2 GPA. That ended my career at Stanford. He explained the way the world worked, and I just about could not believe it. I reminded him that I had one of the fastest times in the nation in the hurdles. He told me that it would make no difference if I were the current world record holder...Stanford University was for scholars first and scholar/athletes next. Athletes, he explained, should check out our fine junior college system. That is how I ended up at Pierce Junior College...my first real dose of real-world reality.

Just to finish up the Stanford story, decades later, at the 2004 U.S. Track and Field Olympic Trials, I got invited to a very special dinner by my old coach at Chapman University, Steve Simmons. Coach Simmons went on to become head manager of the 1980 and 1984 USA Olympic Track and Field Teams and team leader in 1992. He was a star among track coaches in the U.S. and around the world. In 2004, he was in charge of a private dinner at the trials for all of the living U.S. Olympic track coaches and their guests. I had been one of his first NCAA All-Americans and he was kind enough to invite my wife and me to this prestigious event.

The room was filled with my heroes, including Dr. LeRoy Walker. Coach Walker was the first black U.S. Olympic coach of any sport. I was introduced to the crowd. This was a spirited group and so they started peppering me with questions. What did I run? I said I was a sprinter/hurdler and long jumper. There was a long silence. Then one of the black coaches asked me if I was black...a question that got a big round of laughs. I told him that I had been black during my athletic years but changed over to white when I started my business career, for obvious reasons. That too (thankfully) got a really big round of laughs. At that, we were all seated for dinner.

I sat down and greeted the lady on the left of me, Deanne Volchatzer, coach of the 1996 U.S. Olympics Women's Track Team. As I spoke with her, I felt an arm on my shoulder. I turned to greet the person who would be seated to my right and recognized him instantly...Coach Payton Jordan, the long-retired coach of Stanford University, who was now 92 years old. He hugged me, looked me in the eye and said, "Son, (I was 57 years old at the time), how are your grades?" I said, "Coach, they got a lot better." He replied, "Well, that is good, they needed some improvement." He then told me that he had followed my entire track career, kept an eye on me throughout my business career...and that he was very proud of me. It was all I could do to keep from crying.

We had a spectacular night at that dinner. They have a tradition where each Olympic coach stands, introduces himself or herself and mentions the team they coached. They then tell one story from their year as a U.S. Olympic coach.

One coach got up and introduced himself...Jimmy Carnes, coach of the 1980 U.S. Olympic Track and Field Team...the team that never got to compete. President Jimmy Carter chose to politicize the Olympics and boycotted the games, which were held in Moscow, because the Russians had invaded Afghanistan. The coach started to tell the story of being taken out of his house and rushed to the White House to stand near the president as he made the devastating announcement. As he told the story, he choked up and began to weep. How could you ever get over that kind of disappointment? From the looks of it, you could not. An emotional moment for all in the room.

I knew that Coach Jordan had lost his wife recently and that he was currently battling cancer. I had been through my own cancer battle and tried to be of some comfort to him. In true coaching form, he quickly turned the conversation around to me and away from himself. Every great coach I have ever known has that built-in trick...they are totally focused on the success and well-being of others, even if they themselves are hurting. A coach to the end, he died a few years later. I am thankful to God...and to Coach Simmons...for setting up this opportunity to close a circle between a great man and myself...a man I disappointed at one time, but who was happy for whatever success I ended up achieving. Coach Payton Jordan...my hero.

CHAPTER SIX

A Few Mistakes in College...and, Repeat...

Back to my lack of self-discipline, this time in college...

I continued to drink and smoke and run track and live like a wild man for the next two years in junior college. Two buddies and I lived in our own apartment. We drank a beer or two a day...certainly could not afford more. We were so broke that we sold Green Stamps to get money for beer...you will have to look up that old reference. When we did have a few extra bucks or there was a party to attend, I drank to excess...just beer, but lots of beer. However, I was serious enough about track that I do not recall getting in much trouble while drinking, but those around me sure did.

One of my roommates was on the football team and he had the season-ending party at our apartment. The linemen picked up the Coke vending machine and threw it into the pool. That caused a bit of a stir.

By the end of my sophomore year, I was ready to move on to a regular university and to continue my track career. I had several offers and chose Chapman University...best decision of my life.

A week before the start of my junior year...my first year at Chapman...I was with a buddy at his apartment in Torrance Beach, California. We were having a beer when there was a knock on the door. He asked me to answer it. I did. On the other side of the door was an eight-and-a-half-month pregnant young lady. She asked me if Richie was around. I was very happy she had asked for Richie.

Richie had no idea the young lady was pregnant. He immediately suggested they get married...like right now. They did get married just a few days later. I attended the wedding (by the way, that marriage lasted some 50 years, until Richie's recent death). I got plastered at the wedding, went to a topless bar, closed that bar and drove home drunk at 2 a.m. Just about in front of the apartment where I had met Richie's soon-to-be wife, the driver in front of me slammed on his brakes and attempted to turn into a driveway. I hit him so hard that my foot broke off the brake pedal and my foot and ankle shattered.

By the time the police arrived, I was in a lot of pain and out of my car. The people in the car I hit were so drunk that they could not identify who had hit them...even though my car was crushed into the back and side of their car. They were not hurt and that was their house...so the officer let them go home and told me to walk out of there while I still could. I walked several miles home on a badly broken foot and ankle, lucky not to be in a drunk tank somewhere.

I arrived home in time for my parents to just be waking up. I was bloodied, drunk still, in massive pain and had no idea where my crushed-up car was, nor exactly how I had managed to get home (I think the local paper delivery guy gave me a ride part of the way). My dad wanted to go down to the police station and raise hell over my treatment. I suggested that we not do that right now...that I had to be at Chapman University by noon. So, we went to the hospital to get my broken foot and ankle put into a cast and my parents then dropped me off at Chapman with my broken foot, hung over, with no car, just in time for me to accept the one and only athletic full scholarship they had left for that year. The coaches were not pleased.

That afternoon, I met Linda Collins, my future wife. I met her and her new friend...soon to become her forever best friend, Karin May, in the Resident Manager's Office of our dorm. That evening there was a reception for new students. Linda was an incoming freshman and I was a new junior. I made sure I got next to her in line and chatted her up. By the end of the evening, I had managed to ask her out. She agreed. On our first date, I told her I loved her (she replied that I was a "swell date") and told her that I was going to marry her. By summer we were engaged. By the next summer we were married.

CHAPTER SEVEN

But First Some Monkey Business

Not all of my misadventures while drinking involved car accidents and the like... most involved letting things out from inside of me that should never be let out... like a bad temper I can otherwise keep almost completely buried, or bad judgment that gets really bad when I am drunk, or a mean streak that is always right there below the surface, or the afore-documented loss of rational fear and good sense. All those things need to be kept in check...and alcohol provided no checks. So, here is a story that I have never told anyone...in fact, I swore to the other guy involved that I would never tell anyone, but he is now dead, and I am not going to mention his name. Here goes...

The summer before I got married, I had a mindless, boring, poor-paying job at a metal working shop. We left for work at 5:30 a.m. Monday through Friday and got home each day about 6:00 p.m. A couple of my buddies worked with me and we often shared rides. One of those guys shared my idea of relaxation after work, so we hung out almost every night during the week. On the weekends, I was off to my fiancé's parents' house in the San Fernando Valley to spend the break with my soon-to-be wife.

During the week, I would get home from work, take a shower, have a beer and maybe something to eat...I was living at my parents' house for the summer months. I would pick up my buddy and we would go to the Manhattan Beach Pier. We would buy a six-pack along the way and get some bait and head out onto the pier to fish and drink 'til midnight. We were bottom fishing for the halibut that were plentiful back then. Once set up, we would leave our gear there (and no one ever bothered it...we all knew each other) and go catch a jazz set at the Lighthouse

Cafe...a bar just down from the pier...a truly great jazz club in those days. We knew the manager and could listen to a set with or without buying a drink. Then we would go check our lines to see if we had a halibut for dinner the next night. This gave us great down time, wonderful relaxation and a nice buzz. Made the weeks tolerable as I counted down the days to my marriage.

One night, another of our buddies shows up with his fishing pole. Sets up next to us. Starts talking....and talking...and talking...and grabbing one of our beers...and then another...and some of our bait...and talking and talking. After about three nights of this, we had had enough of our freeloading buddy and he was seriously messing with both our buzz and our relaxation. We put together a plan to deal with the situation...and I will say upfront that I am not very proud of the plan...but here it is...

My good friend had an older brother who was a veterinarian. We went to visit him. Asked if he had any dead animals he had yet to dispose of. He did...a full-grown black spider monkey...died earlier in the day and was in the freezer. We asked if we could have him. Sure, no problem. We put the frozen monkey in a bag and off we went.

That night, we set up like normal. Our talkative friend joined us. We finally all headed to the jazz club. While there, I excused myself to go to the bathroom. I then ran to our car, got the thawed-out monkey, ran him out to our fishing poles, reeled in the talkative friend's line, lip hooked the monkey and cast him out into the sea at the end of the Manhattan Beach Pier. I quickly returned to the club, just as the set was ending. Time to go check our lines.

Our friend saw his pole nearly bent in two by the weight of the monkey. It bobbed up and down as the current moved around the dead monkey. He grabbed the pole and fought the monster "fish." As it got to the surface, the lights from the pier revealed a non-fish-looking head, full of dark black hair. "What the fuck?" screamed our friend. This brought everyone at the end of the pier over to the rail.

As the crowd pushed in, our friend kept reeling in the dead, wet monkey. The lights gave it a horrible look as it hung there in space, limp, dripping, and I really hate to say this...looking very much like a hairy child. The crowd went silent. Our friend went silent. He silently kept on reeling it in.

As the monkey got nearly to the rail, the line broke. Eight-pound test line on a fifteen-pound monkey made much heavier by all the wet fur. The monkey plummeted into the waves below. If floated a bit and then disappeared under the pier. We never saw it again.

He told everyone at the end of the pier that he had hooked a child. People disagreed....no, it was a seal....I thought it was just a bunch of seaweed...no, our friend said..."I was two feet from it...it was a hairy child!" Everyone went back to their poles. Our friend packed up and went to his car to grab a flashlight. He spent the next several hours going up and down the beach looking for that poor hairy dead child.

We never saw our friend on the pier after that. I tried to bring it up several times, including at our 40th high school reunion and he DID NOT want to talk about it. I am pretty sure that incident gave him real trauma that has lasted a lifetime. It did, however, keep him out of our bait and beer and restored our relaxation...so it had that going for it.

CHAPTER EIGHT

Naked and Unafraid

I still smoked at Chapman and drank when I could, but I was pretty busy with track and Linda and the occasional visit to a classroom, so I cut back quite a bit on my drinking. When I did have too much to drink, Coach Simmons could always tell, and he would work me out the next day so hard that it pretty much discouraged me from drinking too much next time around.

Linda and I got married in 1969. We were as broke as broke could be. I was making next to nothing working for an insurance company. She was still in school. I had one more semester to go and my scholarship had run out. So, drinking just did not happen very often. It certainly was not a problem or a daily issue. I continued to smoke because I had a class that was off-campus at Marine Corps Air Station El Toro and I could buy cigarettes for 25 cents a pack in the commissary.

Skip forward to the end of my smoking career. Linda and I took a trip during the first year of our marriage to see her grandparents, who lived on Oahu. Her granddad had emphysema and still smoked. He would cough so hard he would nearly pass out. As soon as he stopped coughing, he would light up a cigarette and start the whole cycle over again. I had a history of asthma and could see my future in his coughing fits, and it planted the seed that I needed to quit. In fact, I told Linda that I would quit smoking the day she told me she was pregnant with our first child. Linda got pregnant in 1973, told me the happy news and I reached in my shirt pocket, gave her my half-full hard pack of Marlboros and never ever had another puff. I kept my word and I am thankful to this day that I made that decision. Oddly enough, I was never tempted to have even one more...I knew that I had to have zero tolerance for tobacco, or I would be right back to smoking, because I loved smoking. Now some 45 years later, I miss smoking not at all and I am never tempted to go back to that habit.

As an adult with a wife, eventually two kids, a mortgage and a good job, I calmed down my drinking significantly. I did not drink often, but when I did drink, I often drank too much. And then a few things happened that changed my life...

I got invited to a Rams game at the Coliseum in Los Angeles, corporate seats controlled by a long-time childhood friend. He had become very successful, much more successful than I at that point in our lives. He was also a bit more conservative in his lifestyle. I was pretty much still a wild man back then.

We got to the game and the seats were GREAT. I sat down and a big guy sat down next to me...it was Gomer Pyle...Jim Nabors. Jim could not have been nicer. He told me that he would buy all the beer for us if I would go get it...he would never make it back to his seats if he had to get the beer because of fans wanting autographs and photos. Sounded like a great deal to me and I took him up on it. I made many trips to get the beer...way too many trips on a hot day in the Coliseum.

By the end of the game, I was just completely hammered. We said goodbye to Jim and headed over to Julie's...a great hangout restaurant and bar near the University of Southern California campus in downtown Los Angeles. My host and I went in and ordered something to eat and, oddly enough, more beer. We were seated outside, and it was hot. Our seats were next to the centerpiece of the restaurant...a swimming pool. Julie, the owner, was quite old by then, but she was there greeting everyone...and everyone was there, the place was packed. I think my host was talking with her when I decided to get naked and go for a swim. This was well-received by the packed house and I did several laps, complete with flip turns at each end...before my host pulled me out of the pool and dragged me out to his car... naked and soaking wet. Apparently, I had embarrassed him somehow. I remember clearly hearing the sirens getting closer...I think Julie had called the cops...so as we sped off before they could arrive, I shoved my wet ass out the passenger side window as we passed the entrance of the restaurant and mooned the assembled crowd in a manner that few will ever forget. My host dumped me at home where my bewildered wife tried to figure out why I was asleep and naked and wet after attending a football game. I don't think my host even bothered to tell her...he was out of there. Never heard much from him again.

Woke up the next day, hung over, sunburned, not entirely clear on what had happened the day before and, for the first time, wondering if maybe it might be time for me to kind of move away from alcohol. A person could get in trouble with that stuff.

CHAPTER NINE

Ever Get to See Your Hometown Pharmacist Drunk, Wearing Only a Jock and Dispensing Ice Cubes for Your Drink from that Jock?

I soon had that first idea of moving away from alcohol reinforced. My dad belonged to a group in our hometown…a group of fairly elite businessmen…no women in those days…who met each month for breakfast and some of the cruelest, funniest humor at each other's expense that I had ever heard. When a guest joined for a meeting, they too were torn to pieces. My dad was a member for 65 years and even had me write in his obituary that he had long awaited the reduced dues that that group offered to its deceased members.

I got to go to one of the best ever monthly meetings of the group. The president of a giant oil company was a long-time member. He was a bit tone deaf about the environment. The week before, one of his company's pipelines had leaked a ton of oil onto a beach in Santa Barbara. This gentleman went to the site of the spill and said on live TV…"I don't understand what the big deal is about a few dead birds." That did not play well in Santa Barbara, or anywhere.

The very next weekend the honcho from the oil company shows up as usual at the breakfast meeting. The other members were dressed as oil-covered birds and everything about the meeting centered around the spill…chocolate syrup all over the tables and floor, covering dead fish and dead chickens from the parking lot into the dining room. Two hours of skits and obituaries from the grieving parents of dead seals and birds followed. The honcho sat through all of it…standard fare at these meetings. And you wonder why my sense of humor is a bit warped.

But back to the tie-in with drinking...this group has an annual event that is hard to describe without using unfair words like orgy or drunken brawl. Actually, it was not an actual orgy or an actual brawl, but it kind of looked like it was. I went to several, including my 93-year-old dying dad's last one, to which I carried him not too long ago.

A complete aside...my dad was in the club's band for 65 years, playing guitar or whatever else was needed. As he got older, and the whole band got older, their performances became hard to watch. They never played anything newer than about 1950 vintage. My dad had become hard of hearing. People in the audience would shout out, "You stink!" and dad would reply, "That's right, that was Benny Goodman." Kind of tragic/funny to watch.

Back to the annual event...

It took place outdoors on a golf course and in the surrounding woods. Liquor was served. If you looked closely, you might see a naked woman or two serving drinks...I know because I always looked closely. At my dad's last roundup, I asked two of them if they had any clothes with them, as I wanted to take a photo of my dad with them, but my mom would kill both of us if they were naked. They had bikinis and put them on. I told them to watch themselves because dad had a drink in him. "Dad with a drink in him can get a little handsy," I said. They said, "We don't care." So, I got a great last photo of dad with quite a good smile on his face as he was holding on to each young lady's ass cheeks so he would not fall down... or so he said.

That was a bit traumatizing for me to see, but there was something much, much worse. I had a longtime friend who was the local druggist. I loved this man... respected him...wanted to be like him. When I was a kid, I would drop in to see him each morning on my way to school and he would buy me a Coke or give me a comic book or candy bar and send me on my way. Loved him.

Then one day, when I became an adult, I attended the annual event on the golf course and was wandering down a fairway with a drink in hand, looking for people I might know. Found one. It was Mr. Meese (name changed to protect the guilty)...the pharmacist....my long-time hero. Mr. Meese was wearing...a jock. He had on nothing else. He was an old man by then and this was not a great sight. As I got closer, I could see he was absolutely plastered...and it was about 9 a.m. When I got close enough for him to recognize me, he greeted me warmly and said, "Donny boy...so good to see you. Here, let me cool down that drink for you." At that, he reached into his jock, pulled out a couple of ice cubes and plopped them into my Bloody Mary. I hope to complete my psychiatric counseling within a few more years. Yet another signpost that maybe alcohol could get a person in trouble.

Chapter Ten

Giving the CEO the Finger...a Career-Limiting Gesture

I made officer at the Allstate Insurance Company in 1988. This was a big deal to me and made us financially secure. I was proud of my success and wanted more. Hard to imagine this today, but things were different in the 1980s and 1990s... people drank at company functions, got in their company cars and drove home. That thought is horrifying today and should have been back then, but it was not. I got to witness the end of that era.

It happened for me in two steps. Step one, I went to a celebration dinner with the officers of our division of the company...about a dozen of us. The number two guy was my mentor and close friend and he had a habit of getting behind the president of the company and giving me the finger...since I could do nothing in return. He did this on the way into the dinner and had a big chuckle about it. The president, Bob Leibold, was a great guy...quite religious and a straight shooter. He would have not appreciated this childish play between two of his officers, but it all went on behind his back, so he never saw it.

Bob surprised me that evening. He sat next to me and, after a long while, I noticed that he was quite hammered...drunk as a skunk. I had never seen him drink, much less drunk. I followed his lead and also got drunk. At the end of the evening, I got in my car and the other officers got in theirs and we all drove to our respective homes...most of us quite impaired.

Between the private club where we had dinner in Dundee, Illinois, and my house in Barrington, Illinois, was a stretch of woods and a long lonely four-lane road through those woods. I was driving along in the right-hand lane, trying my best to look and drive like I was sober. In the other lane, I saw a car speeding toward me. It was my buddy, Jim Strohl, the guy who had given me the finger earlier. I prepared my retaliation. When he pulled up alongside me at a red light, I put my arm out the driver's side window, flashed my lights up and down, gave him the finger and pumped my arm around so he could not miss it and kept honking the horn to get his full attention. After 10 or 15 seconds of this, I was pretty pleased with myself and turned to give him a great big smile. Much to my surprise, it was not my friend Jim driving the car. It was Bob Leibold alone, president of our division...President!

Bob looked at me and threw his arms out to the side with a look on his face that said..."What the fuck?" I did the only thing I could think to do—floored the gas pedal and sped away from the scene.

I got home well past midnight, drunk and pretty much hysterical. My wife could not calm me down. I eventually told her the story and let her know that I would be unemployed in the morning. And then I had a horrible thought...in the morning, Bob Leibold and I were flying together to New York City to spend two days calling on insurance brokers and staying at our company condo on the edge of Central Park...nearly three days together *mano a mano.* I slept not one moment that night.

The next day, I got to the airport first and got on the plane. Bob got on and sat down next to me. He did not say a word. When we landed, I got us a cab and we went to drop off our luggage at the condo...no words spoken. We then headed out to see our first broker...still silence between us. The second broker had an in-house chef and we had lunch at their office. More silence. Eventually, our host excused himself to take a call and Bob asked to speak to me out on the balcony overlooking NYC. I was not sure if he was going to push me over the railing or just fire me. Once we got outside, he said, "Don...I was so drunk last night that I have no recollection of what I said or did to you to make you so mad as to violently give me the finger. In fact, I could not sleep a wink...I am just sick that I must have acted WAY out of line. So, I want to sincerely apologize and ask for your forgiveness...and if you can find it in your heart to give me that forgiveness, let's just put this behind us and never talk about it again." Alrighty then...

That was the first moment that told me it was time to put away the alcohol... that I was getting too high up the chain to make that kind of mistake, and that I would never get that lucky again.

Next up was a similar party where the president of the entire company was involved in a car accident on the way home from a corporate dinner. People were hurt. The president had apparently been drinking. The story made headline news around the country, due to his high position in one of America's biggest insurance companies. I also noted that his career came to an end not too long after that incident. It made a big impression on a lot of us. Time for America to grow up and get serious about not driving while intoxicated...way past time. Time for me to grow up, as well.

CHAPTER ELEVEN

The One and Only Physical Fight I Have Ever Had with My Wife

***Yet another...*"here are the reasons I quit drinking" story.**

The family and I moved to Pittsburgh so I could run an insurance office there. I had never been to Pittsburgh. Knew no one there. Knew nothing about it. What I did know was not necessarily positive...old decaying steel-working town. Well, parts of that might have been true, but it turned out to be one of the best places to live and work ever. I love Pittsburgh.

We had lots of adventures and fun in Pittsburgh. I got to crawl around in deep, below-ground coal mines, accidentally fall into rusty cold water ponds while trying to play golf, watch amazing fights in the stands at Cleveland versus Pittsburgh football games, see my son get into a fight at a Pirates baseball game...a bit about that one....

The Pirates were in trouble financially when we were living in Pittsburgh. The owners were on the verge of having to sell the team. So, we did all we could to support them and attended maybe 45 games one year. The crowds were so thin that I got something like ten foul balls one game...didn't have to fight for them, just walked over and picked them up.

So, one of these games actually had a bit of a crowd...the stadium was maybe one-third full...a good turnout for that year. My son, Jim, was about ten at the time, and I, not being all that good a parent, would let him and his friend wander off to do whatever they wanted at the ball park ("Just be back here by the eighth inning, Jim, we might want to get an early start home.")

At one point in the game, I see a disturbance in the expensive seats down near the field on the third base side. I get out my binoculars and check it out. In the middle of the melee...my son and his friend beating the dickens out of two other kids for reasons unknown. The fight was soon broken up and the security people grabbed the other two kids, who probably actually had seats in that section, while Jimmy and his friend ran for it. I went back to eating my hot dog and watching the game.

Jimmy and the friend returned by the eighth inning. They never said a word about the fight. I did not inquire...again, probably a good indicator of my not-so-good parenting skills. I learned years later that they were fighting over a foul ball... so at least it was something worth fighting over.

OK...so I am avoiding getting to the point of the physical fight featuring my wife, Linda, and me.

We got invited to a pretty nifty event. The president of the alumni association of the local university, the University of Pittsburgh, invited us to join him for free at the annual alumni dinner honoring him for his service. I was sure this was a big fund-raising event and soon found that to be true. When we arrived, we were taken to Table Number One, where our friend and his wife were already seated. They introduced us to the chancellor of the university, the sportscaster for the local TV station, the manager of the Pirates and on and on...the elite of Pittsburgh. This was going to be quite a night.

The meal was gourmet. The drinks and wine were all but forced down our throats. Linda got hammered early...maybe only the second time in our lives together that I had ever seen her drunk. She was so drunk that she snuck out of the dinner and disappeared. I finally went looking for her. I found her passed out in the back seat of our car, which was parked on a dark city street in a tough neighborhood...doors not locked.

I got her out of the car and walked her back to safe territory. I then walked her around for another fifteen minutes or so until she said she was now alright and could return to the dinner. We went back in.

By now dinner was over, after-dinner drinks were being served, and the local celebrities were all around us, delighting us with story after story. More drinks were served. And before long, Linda was not the problem. I was probably as drunk as I had ever been in my life...and that was saying something.

And then it began...the auction. So here I am, at the head table. I have been introduced all around to people who had actually done something in their lives and mattered...as the big head dog of a prestigious insurance company...truth being I was a branch manager of a small office of a startup insurance company owned by a prestige company...and I was not the filthy rich guy that our host told everyone I was. But it all sounded good to me, so I was ready to play the role of rich guy and drunk enough to make it look real.

I bought everything. I outbid the mayor, for God's sake. I outbid Chuck Noll, maybe the greatest coach of all time, on a first-class trip for four anyplace in the world that U.S. Air (now Delta) flew...and Coach Noll just looked over at me and shook his head. I was on a roll.

When everything was over, I gave someone a credit card or two and paid for everything. We then got into my car and I worked the steering wheel while Linda worked the peddles to get us home...thankful and ashamed to this day for driving home drunk some 40 years ago...but I did...and somehow made it.

When we got home, neither Linda nor I could figure out how to open the garage door...that ought to tell you why I am thankful I injured no one on the way home. It was really cold out and there was snow on the ground. I insisted she get out of the car to get the garage door figured out and open. She tried, with no success. I berated her for her inept attempt to do something simple like open a garage door. That was not received well. Words were exchanged. Next thing I know, I am out of the car coming at her. Linda starts swinging. I should mention that we were both trained in karate...never made it too high up the "belts" ranks, but we both know how to fight properly. Her swinging—and eventually mine—involved none of that training. She and I were both cold, drunk, frustrated and boiling mad. We flailed at each other for several minutes in the snow, with the serious intent of bringing about bodily harm, but without the ability to do so. No blow was ever landed. We eventually gave up and acted like nothing had happened...our one and only and physical fight ever...shameful.

Once inside the house...we had to leave the car in the snow and go in the front door...we immediately went to bed and to sleep.

The next day we woke up simultaneously, horribly hung over and with the startled realization that we may have done something stupid the night before. I ran outside to see if the car was damaged...to see if I was in real trouble. No, the car was fine, but still running and nearly out of gas. I went back inside, and a few memories of the night before started to drift into my head. Oh shit...I think I bought some stuff. I called the credit card company. That card was maxed out. I called my back-up card company...maxed out as well. Oh double shit!

We then tried to recall what we might have bought. Oh...that was painful. The items would come into my head slowly...oh damn, here comes one...a pair of football cleats signed by a player I, and probably no one else, had ever heard of...oh no...I think I paid $500 for them.

A trip around the world first class for four...oh that one was going to hurt...and it did when I saw what I had paid.

On and on...one piece of shit after another, each one bought at an outrageous price by Linda or myself.

And then I remembered a really odd one. It was four opened and empty beer cans from four different breweries I had never heard of. I think the program (which I had lost on the way home along with all the receipts) said it they were somehow collectible. I could not remember how much I had paid for them, but I was sure I had won the bidding and recalled that I knocked out the competition with an extremely generous bid right off the bat...could not remember how much. I called the university and finally found someone who could tell me how much I had paid and what I had bought. I had bought the collection and paid a thousand dollars for it...for four empty beer cans.

I told her I would be down to pick them up later that afternoon. She said, no need, she will send a truck up with the cans. I asked why they would send a truck for four cans. She explained that I had not bought four cans, I had bought a collection of empty beer cans large enough to fill an entire two-ton truck. They were delivered that afternoon. I'm guessing the total value must have approached ten dollars...a truckload of stinky, empty beer cans.

All this happened more than 30 years ago. I am now 73 years old and living in Hawaii. I still get invited to this and every other charity auction in Pittsburgh...to this day. Reason number...well, I have lost count, as to why I quit drinking.

CHAPTER TWELVE

A Signed Contract Not to Drink

About that time, my two kids came home from high school one day. They were upset because they were being required to sign a contract in order to be allowed to play on their respective athletic teams. The contract said they would not drink during the season...no exceptions. I told them to sign it...no big deal...they were too young to drink anyway. Now, my kids were pretty direct with Linda and me about most things, so they both blurted out that they would have a beer at a party from time to time and had no intention of stopping. I said that they could easily give that up for a few months and just to sign the contract and not drink. They countered with... "You couldn't do it." At that, I took one of the contracts, went upstairs and made a copy of it, filled in my name, signed and dated it and gave it back to them. I told them I would stop drinking entirely until their season was over. At that, they signed the contracts...I have no idea if they avoided drinking altogether, but they at least pretended to and neither of them ended up with substance abuse problems later in life.

I made it through the next several months without a drink. I found I felt better than I had in a long time. I lost some weight. I started running marathons again. I never had those headaches the next day after business dinners. I gave no president the finger. Life was good. That was about 30 years ago...and I have never had a single beer, glass of wine or other drink since then...not once. I do huff paint....no, just kidding.... I am drug-, alcohol- and tobacco-free for the rest of my life. But I am not a crusader asking you to follow my lead...people make their own decisions. I also recognize that quitting is not as easy for some as I have described it was for me. In fact, those who end up in AA or rehab to change their habits have my utmost respect. Addiction is a bitch.

So...that is why I quit drinking. I did it for self-preservation and for the good of my family...and for my own health. I did it because it used to get me into trouble, and I worked too hard to piss it all away because I made a stupid mistake while drunk. I did it because I have people I care about deeply who have lost loved ones to drunk drivers...probably drivers who were no more drunk than I was on many occasions behind the wheel. I did it because I got some breaks that I did not deserve, and I certainly did not deserve any further breaks. I did it because I felt I had run out of good luck and needed to concentrate on doing the right thing rather than having people bail me out when I got in trouble. I did it for me. And I am thankful to God that I did.

When I look back on it all, I realize I was probably not an alcoholic...I was never addicted to alcohol and could go long months without anything to drink at all. But no matter, I was a problem drinker and the problems might have been infrequent, but they were significant. In the insurance business you talk about losses in terms of frequency and severity. My problem was not one of frequency... but it sure as hell was one of severity. I am so thankful that the only one I ever really harmed was me...but that was just by pure luck. So many incidents could have ended tragically and I am not sure I could have handled the guilt. Mistakes were made, but the current state feels damn good. I'm not always proud of my past, but I am quite proud of my present. Life is good.

Get help if you need it...and now will be better than later. No shame in getting help...we could all use some from time to time.

CHAPTER THIRTEEN

Working for My Complete Opposite

No one I have ever worked with at Allstate or Northbrook Property and Casualty Insurance would ever guess that I could put together an entire chapter of stories about Bob Leibold. Well, guess again, because here it comes.

I was working for both Allstate and Northbrook in South Barrington, Illinois.

Bob was hired by Allstate Insurance to start up a new company that would seek to gain the business insurance of independent agents and brokers. Allstate agents controlled very little of that business and Allstate wanted it. So, instead of buying an existing commercial lines company (and several were given heavy consideration) the thought was to build our own company and avoid any unknown long tail legacy that an existing company might unknowingly have...like asbestos, lead paint or tobacco claims that could emerge decades later.

Bob was from CNA Insurance out of Pennsylvania. He was a nice-looking (in a kind of cleaned-up Abe Lincoln-looking way) tall guy with an easy smile and a direct approach. Humor was not his main strength.

Bob built a company that was consistently voted as the one providing the best service to its independent agents and brokers and their clients of any company in the industry. Bob also took on responsibility for the insurance policies for small commercial businesses that Allstate agents wrote, the large national accounts that were largely a hold-over from our days of being owned by Sears Roebuck and our reinsurance company. It all totaled up to a billion dollars in annual premiums, not a small number, but peanuts compared to the huge premiums written by the rest of Allstate. We were highly regarded in the industry, but really seen as only a bit of distraction to the rest of the Allstate family of companies. I used to say that if Allstate were to have a family dinner, we would be at the kid's table in the corner.

I want to make this clear right now.... I HIGHLY respected Bob Leibold, admired him, appreciated him and kept him as my friend throughout his long life. I was extremely sad when he passed away recently in his 90s. He served our company well...grew a business from scratch that we were later able to sell for good money...and volunteered for big jobs with his church throughout his retirement years. Bob was a first-class human being.

That said, Bob could be just a little bit tight with the dollar and his sense of humor was...pretty much missing at work. And I could drive him absolutely nuts...

CHAPTER FOURTEEN

Fresh Raspberries in NYC

Bob and I decided to go to NYC to call on national brokers home-officed there. I thought that traveling with the president of a big company would be glamorous and told my wife that I would be taking my first trip on the corporate jet. No... we took United...economy seats. When we arrived in NYC, we got our bags at baggage and we then went outside to wait for a bus...that is right...a bus...to take us from the Newark Airport in New Jersey to the Port Authority Bus Terminal, the fabulous main bus station in NYC. A bus. Once we arrived, Bob instructed me to grab my luggage and we walked to the company condo...quite a long walk dragging a piece of luggage. He explained that cabs were expensive in the city and that he always walked. To tell the truth, his thrifty ways were getting on my nerves.

The next morning, I got up early and went for a 10-mile run in Central Park...I was in training for a marathon. By about 7 a.m., I had returned, showered and gotten ready for the day, and met Bob in the dining room of our condo location, which was the old Essex House right next to Central Park...an elegant and expensive location. Time for breakfast.

The waiter gave us menus. When he returned, I ordered a tall orange juice, bacon, eggs, toast and coffee. Bob ordered dry cereal and plain tap water. He then suggested that I try the dry cereal, that the Essex House was known for its excellent Rice Krispies. I understood exactly what he meant...the food I had ordered was too damn expensive. I told him I had just run ten miles and was starving...since we had skipped dinner entirely the night we arrived. I affirmed my order to the waiter. Bob was fuming. He pulled up a newspaper loudly and snapped it in front of his face...that was the end of our breakfast conversation.

When my meal arrived, it looked excellent...and it was. When his meal arrived, it looked like Rice Krispies...and it was. Plain Rice Krispies in a sea of milk and nothing else, not even coffee. I could almost see the steam coming out of Bob's ears. I offered him a piece of toast...no reply.

The waiter tried to defuse the situation. He told Bob that his cereal looked a little plain, would he like a few fresh raspberries on top? Bob thought that was a great idea and had him heap on the raspberries. And it did seem to defuse the situation--we both got what we wanted. Until...

Until the bill arrived. Bob's fresh raspberries added $45 to his bill...that would be $45 in 1990s money. Apparently, raspberries were out of season in the U.S. and these had been flown in first class from someplace like a hidden valley in Tibet and then chauffeured from the airport in a high-end Mercedes.

Bob just stared at the bill and then he tried to hide it from me. I asked to see it. No need, he said, he would put it on his card. He put down the bill and his card and we waited for the waiter. I could not stand the suspense, so I reached over and picked up the bill and saw the charge. I have never laughed harder or longer in my life...and Bob was red-faced and as mad at me as he had probably ever been at any human being. His Rice Krispies, with berries and plain water, came to ten dollars more than my full meal. If you know me at all, you know for sure that I NEVER let Bob forget that meal.

CHAPTER FIFTEEN

Get Rid of the Shrimp and the Piano Player

Over the years Bob and I got along great. He respected what I did, and I respected him. However, we fought over petty expenses all the time. I would put together an event in Bermuda and he would ask me to come in to review it with him before we left town. He would go through each item and ask questions like, "How much are those shrimp...each?" I would look and answer, "Well, Bob, agents love shrimp, and these are our best producers, so let's not get into the pieces discussion here, I am bringing this event in under budget." That never flew. He would persist... "How much...each?" He would finally drag it out of me...they were a bit pricey at $4.50 each...and I had ordered about a 1000 of them for our several hundred guests. "Scratch the shrimp!" he commanded. I shook my head, did not say a thing and scratched the shrimp...except I did not scratch the shrimp, I am not an idiot. Agents love shrimp.

When the big event arrived, the agents loved the shrimp and the event was a big hit. Bob never mentioned the shrimp again.

On another occasion, I had brought in a pianist to play softly in the background at a reception. The reception was a big hit....or so I thought. The next day, Bob called me into his office. I thought I was going to get a pat on the back. What he had in mind was a bit lower. He asked me whose idea it was to have a pianist at the reception. I told him it was mine. He then asked how much it cost. I told him. Now, I am not sure I had ever before heard Bob cuss or say a harsh thing to anyone, but that was about to change on this particular morning. He told me that I had wasted the company's money. That his hearing was not as good as it used to be (boy, can I relate to that now!) and the music had made it difficult for him and his then number two guy at the time, Hugh Gaynor....who had a bit of a hearing problem...to hear the conversation of the agents. He then said, and I quote, "If you ever hire a piano player for a company event in the future, I will grab the candelabra off of the piano and shove it up your ass."

I broke out laughing. I don't think any statement in my life had shocked me more than hearing these words come from kind Bob Leibold. And, they were the clearest and most informative words of direction I ever got from him. I laughed until I had a bit of an asthma attack. Bob gave me his best Abraham Lincoln serious look for about five seconds and then he too started laughing. When we were done and he had regained his composure and I had had a hit from my asthma medicine and was no longer laughing and wheezing, he asked me if his instructions were clear. "Crystal," was my reply. No more piano players at any company event...ever.

Chapter Sixteen

**My Brilliant Design for a Marketing Giveaway...
an Insurance Company Condom with the Sears Tower
Showing on One Side of the Condom and the President
of the Company's Face Printed on the Reservoir End**

(I'm guessing you are going to read this chapter...that is the second-best chapter title I have ever put together, surpassed only by Chapter Eleven of my last book... titled, "Turd Drops Three Stories into Circle of Friends.")

I had several other odd moments with Bob. Our beloved marketing assistant vice president was retiring and I was taking his place. Two things happened during that transition. The first was that any significant marketing expenditure I might want to make had to be vetted by Jim Strohl, who by then had become the number two guy in the organization. That kind of irritated me because I was respectful of the company's money and did not feel that I needed to be supervised. Bob felt differently. Now, Jim had been my direct boss for a long time and was my good friend. Jim has a sense of humor. So I thought I would try it out.

I put together an order for an agent "giveaway" item that we might use at events like golf tournaments or for booths at conventions or goodie bags. It was for $50,000 worth of condoms in Northbrook Property and Casualty green (Pantone Matching System 345, if I recall) with the white outline of the Sears Tower on the side of the condom. At the very tip, on the reservoir end, was a drawing of Bob Leibold's face. I filled in the paperwork and waited until after everyone had left the office to put it second item down in Jim Strohl's paperwork in bin. I put it there because I certainly did not want to offend his executive assistant who might see it as she was taking papers in to him, just wanted to mildly protest this ridiculous signing requirement and get a bit of a chuckle out of my buddy, Jim.

I could hardly wait for the next day. Eight o'clock and no mention of the phony order. Nine a.m...maybe he is in a meeting. Ten a.m., he is never this slow; I wonder what is going on. Eleven a.m., I get a call to come in and see Bob Leibold.

Now keep in mind that this is my first day on the job as the new marketing AVP for our division. I head into Bob's office and he is surveying my drawing of the unrolled condom with the Sears Tower and the face on the end of it. Apparently, Jim had signed the request without reading it, so it went to Bob, who did.

I was quite unprepared to answer his questions about the condom order. He looked at it in silence and then looked at me. He asked what the hell he was looking at. I told him that agents had been asking for years for something useful instead of the normal pens and paper weights that companies usually gave out...and that they had specifically asked repeatedly for condoms... a complete and utter lie made up on the spur of the moment. Pretty good lie, because it stopped him completely for a moment. He then said, "Whose face is that on the tip of the condom?" I explained that it was Jim Strohl's face and that part was a joke for Jim only and it would not appear on the final product. He bought it. He then asked why I had put the Sears Tower on the side of the condom. I explained that all of us old Allstaters were proud of the Sears Tower (Sears owned us at the time) and that the agents saw it as a symbol of our strength. The look on his face was priceless. I could tell that he believed every single thing that I had told him. I could also tell that he had absolutely no idea of how to deal with the likes of me. So he rolled up my drawing and handed it and the paperwork back to me and thanked me for my inventiveness, but said that he felt it was inappropriate for our company image and to come up with something else. End of story. That was my first day on the job as our chief marketing officer...quite a day.

Bob Leibold... I am thankful for the time I spent with him. He was a terrific man, a good leader and a heck of a fine human being...and he looked terrific on the tip of a condom.

CHAPTER SEVENTEEN

The Misspelling of "Excellence"

I worked for Allstate Insurance for something like 28 years. I loved Allstate. They treated me well. They trained me well, including sending me out for a condensed graduate level semester at Harvard Business School, same at Kellogg School of Management at Northwestern University, sent me to Disney to learn how they treat their customers like royalty, to Crosby Quality College to learn the process for actually solving problems rather than finding someone to blame, and to several management and leadership courses that changed my life in very positive ways. I loved Allstate.

But then two things happened. One, it became apparent that my steady rise to the top of the corporation had stalled. Second, Allstate sold the part of the company where I worked, and that had serious implications for me.

Long before the sale of my part of the company, I had already started looking for a new job.

I hooked up with one of the great headhunters...I mean executive recruiters... in the entire insurance industry. The guy was legendary, really difficult to deal with and demanding as heck. We not only got along, we became good friends. And he got me ready for my eventual move.

He had a quid pro quo for finding a position for me...I had to help him out first. How? By going out on an interview at a company I was not going to like. Why? To provide me with some practice interviewing at the CEO direct-report level and to show up as a good candidate for a job he was having trouble filling. He told me he would understand if I did not take the job, but that if I was unwilling to "waste my time" traveling to California and spending two days there in the interview process...to prepare myself for better opportunities down the road and to help him out...we were not going to do business. I went.

Allstate was huge and first-class. The company I was interviewing with was small and a specialty insurer...they only sought one kind of commercial customer... let's say agricultural businesses, just to give the niche a name. They were in a secondary city in California and I had never heard of them. But off I went.

I did learn a couple of things. The proposed pay for a much smaller job than I currently had was about 50% more than I was currently making. The title was three levels up from my current title. Everybody at the C level of the company... the level reporting directly to the CEO...the level I was interviewing for...got a company Mercedes S550...quite an upgrade from the Volvo I had at Allstate.

The home office of this new company almost made me cry. It was pitiful. Photos in the lobby of farm scenes were under glass with bright lights on them and the lights had apparently been on them 24/7 for decades. The photos were just smeared blotches of color where you could maybe make out a tractor or bale of hay. Inattention to detail...this would never happen at Allstate.

I asked about the corporate jet. Well, they served one state only, so there was no corporate jet. There was, however, a four-wheel drive pool Jeep you could borrow if you needed to go out on a ranch and did not want to get cow turds on your nifty Mercedes.

I asked one of the top dogs who in the company handled their reinsurance... insurance companies often lay off part of their risk with reinsurance companies so no one huge loss ruins the company, the risk is spread. The top dog said he was unfamiliar with the term, reinsurance. That was not a good sign.

I interviewed with the CEO and each of his direct reports...all male and all white. That would never fly at Allstate (it would have when I first joined that company in 1969, but they got smart quick and did an excellent job of creating and maintaining a diverse staff).

One of those direct reports was a guy I knew by reputation. I am still in touch with him to this day. He was/is a bright guy who had probably come to a stagnation point in his career at the Chubb Insurance Company and had made a career move to this California company. Chubb had a reputation of being a bit East Coast snobby...they hired guys and gals from Ivy League Schools. Allstate hired (in those days) from state colleges. This company, based on the people I had met so far, hired from an agricultural junior college where they had studied milk churning and how to grow wheat. Most of them did not appear to have studied much business or insurance. This ex-Chubb guy had...he was a smart insurance guy.

The interview with the ex-Chubb guy was kind of weird. I got the feeling that he was desperate for another real insurance guy to join him...that person being me. He spent most of the time bragging on the new Mercedes and the title and what a great guy the CEO was (and he was). He tried to make the company look as good as possible, to the point that I suspected he was still trying to justify in his mind why the hell he was now working there. At one point, he told me that the motto of the company was "Striving for excellence." He gave me his business card, which had the motto printed at the bottom. You guessed it... "Excellence" was misspelled...as "Excelence."

I spotted the misspelling immediately and knew he had never noticed it. And then an absolutely delightful thing happened. I noticed that they had also misspelled "Executive" on the card. Under his name on the card was his official title..."Ecutive Vice President." He had also failed to spot that typo.

By now I had absolutely made up my mind that I would not be moving to a secondary city in California to borrow the company four wheeler to skip across cow turds for a living. So I decided to have some fun with the poor guy. I asked him to tell me more about the meaning behind the motto: "Striving for Excellence." He launched into a long story about attention to detail and how, as a relatively small company with world-class talent, they had the time and expertise to get everything just right. I asked them who did their spelling. He gave me a really odd look. I did not say a word...I slid his company card over to him and pointed at "Excelence." He turned bright red. He could barely look me in the eye. He was a Chubb guy, and this was some bull shit. How dare someone embarrass him like this? But I was not through. He finally blurted out "typo" and, I am sure, wanted to move the discussion in another direction. Not me. He had thrown the card in the garbage, but he had one of those old-fashioned card holder things that people have when they are trying to impress you with their title...had it right there on his desk. So, I reached over, got a new card, slipped it to him, pointed to "Ecutive Vice President" and said, "Typo two." That pretty well wrapped up that interview.

I did not get the job. However, the owner of the company was a part owner of a much bigger and more sophisticated specialty insurer in New York City...and pretty soon I found myself sitting in the World Trade Center talking to their head guy. The job came with no car, but we did have a company 737 and they spelled everything right on my business card. I was off to NYC.

CHAPTER EIGHTEEN

Living and Working in NYC

I left Allstate in 1996 after 28 years there, all of them happy. We were family, I still hear from my Allstate friends. I started at the very bottom as an hourly wage "punch the clock" clerk and made my way up to a financially secure officer of the company. I would have stayed to the end except fate stepped in.

Several things happened that caused me to leave Allstate. It became apparent to me that my rise to the top of that company had come to either a plateau or a stop just about the time I hit 50 years of age. Next, Allstate decided to sell the part of the company that I was in, with me included in the package. Third, I got an offer I could not refuse...a job in NYC working for a guy I loved, Pennington Way III, at double my Allstate salary...that was DOUBLE my salary. I found out soon that the increased pay would be needed to support the huge rent on my NYC apartment, but nonetheless, it was a career move forward.

NYC was a brave new world for Linda and me. We had always lived in the suburbs, never in an urban environment. But the idea of commuting each day to work in NYC did not appeal to me, so we looked for an apartment close to the office in downtown NYC...one near the World Trade Center. We found a quite nice three-bedroom apartment down the street from the towers. It had all the storage space of a mid-sized Marriott hotel room. It was less than a quarter the size of our house in Chicago. The rent was $5000 a month...about three times my monthly house payment in Chicago...just to rent.

We sold our cars...you don't need them in Manhattan. We sold many of our worldly goods...sold the piano, sold the weightlifting equipment, sold the gas-powered lawn mower and on and on. We put some stuff in storage and moved a few things into the apartment. The kids had moved out of the house, so it was just Linda and me. Honestly, I loved it. It was kind of like being newlyweds again. No home maintenance and few chores. We went out to dinner 365 nights a year and found plenty to do. My favorite cousin and his fabulous wife lived at Midtown and Penn Way, two buildings from us. My walk to work was a couple of blocks. Life was good.

Chapter Nineteen

Muggers, Buggers and Bono

It was my first day in the office. We were near the top of a high-rise building on Water Street in downtown NYC. I introduced myself to everyone and went into my overly nice office to organize it. About a half hour later, one of my employees came in and asked if I had been briefed on purse thefts in the building. I had not. She then pointed to a nice-looking guy in a dark suit and basketball sneakers who was wandering through the office picking up purses...he had at least three on his arm. I saw him. He saw me. The race was on. I flew across the office floor with all the ladies yelling for me to catch the thief. He just barely beat me to the elevator and was gone.

I found one of the useless guards and asked if security had any video surveillance in the elevators so we could get a good look at the guy. They did. They immediately recognized him as Gus...one of several known purse thieves in the area. We watched the tape as he descended toward the lobby. During the ride, he stripped the purses of cash and cards and shoved them up above the ceiling tiles of the elevator. We quickly retrieved them and got them back to the owners. Then I opened up the petty cash drawer to compensate the victims. We had new rules on purse storage after that morning.

I went for a long jog that evening. It was summer in NYC; the sun was still up, and it was warm. I jogged all the way down to Greenwich Village on the West side and found a pier jutting out into the Hudson River. I jogged out onto the pier... quickly noticing it was not like most other piers I had ever been on. I had on short running shorts and running shoes. The other people there had nothing on. It was a gay guy nude pier, and everyone seemed happy to see me. I don't give one damn about what people do with their sexuality, so I just kept running...until I spotted an older man seated on the ground behind a barrier. He looked like an older banker, pleasant smile, balding head, eyes firmly locked on me. As I got closer, he stood up. He was wearing nothing but a white cloth diaper with diaper pins. That was enough for me. I headed home.

The next morning, Linda and I had a mandatory street safety meeting with a retired NYPD officer whom the company had hired for people like us...new to NYC. He scared us half to death. He told Linda to keep her purse under "her outermost garment"...hidden out of sight. Told me to not interfere with any interaction between a gunman and a store owner...no problem, I would resist that temptation. The very next day, at noon, on Water Street in downtown NYC, I saw a thief come running out of a store with a store owner in close pursuit...in a sea of people heading off to lunch. The owner fired off two rounds at the thief, who was in the middle of all those people. No one was hit, but it certainly got my full attention.

I LOVED NYC. My life there was like a movie script. We went everywhere, did everything...it was all magic. One of my employees, Cecelia Abraham, came into my office one day and said, "Come with me." I asked where we were going. She told me to shut up and follow her (Cecelia can be pretty direct). We got into a cab and went to the very first K-Mart ever in NYC. Her brother was the manager of that new store, which was just opening. He ushered us in to a stage where a dozen people were gathered around a band. This is when I figured out that NYC was different from any other place I had ever lived. The band was U2 and right there was Bono...who greeted me warmly. The band then launched into four songs for us before moving to an outside stage for a free concert to promote their K-Mart sponsored tour, The Popmart Tour.

Almost every day was like that. If you live in NYC you see celebrities all the time. You see street interactions...good and bad...all the time. Your senses are overwhelmed by the humanity, the smells, the excitement of it all. Anything you can think of you can have delivered to your apartment at 1:47 in the morning or 6:22 at night or any other time you wish. The restaurants are endless and diverse. The entertainment is the same. The people are from all over the world. And once you learn the rules of the city, it all kind of works...at least it did back then. Subways work. Cabs work. Walking works. You can time things so you don't try to show up when the crowds are the worst. There are free things to enjoy everywhere. It is an amazing place.

One of those free things was the Staten Island Ferry. It was in easy walking distance from our apartment in Battery Park. In the summertime, you could get on the ferry and it would take you past the Statue of Liberty and over to Staten Island. The ride back took you around the Statue of Liberty again and ahead of you was the sunset skyline of Manhattan...breathtaking. The cost...zero...free public transportation.

NYC is also a hub to the world. I quickly learned that I could fly to London and back on a new airline...new in those days...Virgin Air...for $225 round trip. It was cheaper than flying to someplace like Chicago. So Linda and I would sometimes fly to London for the weekend.

We could walk to Brooklyn, and often did, for dinner or breakfast. We could walk to Soho or Little Italy...which we loved. We learned about street scams and imitation goods. A great example...a guy selling high-end video decks out of the back of his car on Wall Street on the day before Christmas. These were VHS machines...that will tell you it was a couple of decades ago...unopened, from Sears, top of their line...selling for $100...originally priced at over $600. Obviously stolen or shoplifted, but no one seemed to care. He sold out in no time. One guy who worked for me bought one. He showed it to me the day after we returned from Christmas break. He had wrapped it and given it to his new wife's parents as their Christmas gift. They opened it together on Christmas Day. Inside the box...two bricks...no VHS. This guy showed me the bricks and said it did not play out well for him on Christmas Day.

We also learned about NYC pricing...not necessarily dishonest, but you had to be a bit careful with it. Example--my wife and I took two great employees, Cecelia and Carol, out for a celebration dinner. The place we went was owned by a known mob guy and I saw him there often until his eventual arrest. Loved his restaurant...but you had to be a bit cautious. Both Cecelia and Carol ordered the lobster. For the first time in my entire life I said, "Choose something else, you are not having the lobster." But the lobster is on special and it is only $69...a bargain price in NYC. Well, this was going onto my expense account and I actually cared about the company's money, so I pointed out the fine print to them. The lobster was only $69...a pound...and the smallest lobster they had was three pounds. Each of those "bargains" was going to cost over $200 and I would have none of it. By the way...this was not a restaurant where you would want to argue with the waiter about the bill...trust me.

Cecelia is an accomplished woman...highly educated, speaks French beautifully, is a true expert in insurance and NYC suave. She is one of Linda and my best friends and we love her dearly. She is, however, quite different from my Allstate friends. We rarely cussed or told stories or discussed other people on a personal basis at Allstate. Those were not necessarily the same rules in effect in NYC. My first day on the job there, Cecelia, whom I had just met and who was a direct report to me, accompanied me to a meeting with a NYC insurance broker. This guy picked up right away that I was not a true New Yorker and he decide to work me over verbally. Cecelia jumped in and about tore the tongue out of his head...verbally. She used words I had only read about in books...books my parents hid from me. I was very impressed...and I knew I was no longer at Allstate.

At Allstate, we also had a culture that was pretty much devoid of anything that might be sexual or demeaning in nature...of course that is not entirely true, but we were "woke" before the alarm clock went off. Again, not so true in NYC. I remember one of the women who worked for me commenting on one of our lawyers who had paraded around at an off-site meeting in his Speedo. I was aghast that he would do that at a company meeting. I wanted more details. I asked just exactly the wrong question... "How did he look?" She fired back that he looked like he was concealing a roll of dimes. I about died. I was, indeed, no longer at Allstate.

My boss in NYC, Pennington Way III, was one of the best people I have ever been around. We worked with a bunch of characters at our insurance company in NYC, which was owned by a man who was a notorious billionaire with a 737 for a company plane.

Some of these characters were brilliant and top-of-the-line insurance and business people. Some were just...characters. One guy had a snap-on toupee, wore a corset all the time, had teeth that would blind you and wore so much gold jewelry he could have been a rapper. He had sexually harassed half the women in New York. I had no idea how he kept his job, particularly since I believe he was a complete idiot. But he did provide me with my best laugh while working for that company...

Penn and I went to a large insurance conference in Atlanta known as RIMS...a big deal insurance convention. Lots of high-level people from our company attended. We had just bought some company in the UK and their head person attended this meeting. All of our people gathered prior to a cocktail party we sponsored with the idea of introducing ourselves to the new guy. The guy with the snap-on toupee takes over the meeting. He asks each of us to stand and take one minute to introduce ourselves to the new guy and tell him what we do. All of us did exactly what he asked...while wondering why this fool was put in charge of this meeting. When we had all finished, Snap-on Boy gets up and gives a 15-minute presentation on the boring business that he runs and then launches into another five minutes about his long and powerful relationship with the new guy. He says things like...

"Derek and I have known and respected each other for the past three decades and he is like a brother to me."

"The last time Derek was at my house in NYC, we drank enough wine and chased enough women to make for a great movie."

"Derek's oldest son is my godson and I think of him as family."

Five minutes of this, and then Derek gets up...

Derek says, and I quote, "My name is Reginal. I have never been known as Derek in my entire life. I have no son. I do not know this man, other than the fact that he grabbed me as I walked into this meeting. I am assuming that you are all in on this and that there is a camera somewhere recording it." At that he waved to all four corners of the room, as if to catch the camera in one of them, and left. That was his welcome to our fine company.

There was no restoring the meeting after that mess. We laughed Snap-on Boy out of the room and found our way to the bar. Like I said...an idiot.

We had a guy with the same title as me...with a bigger office than mine...with no papers or manuals in that office...with a $3000 suit wrapping his 400-pound body, and no one could tell me exactly what he did for a living...including him. I was told, quietly, that he had something to do with collecting money from those who owed us money. I inquired no further.

There were other oddities in NYC. My first week on the job, a guy comes into my office while I am on the phone and starts measuring me...as I am talking on the phone. I finally stop and ask him what the hell he is doing. He tells me he is measuring me for a tux. I told him I did not need a tux. He told me that the company was buying me two tuxedos and that I would need them in NYC. A day later, two beautiful tuxes arrive...no charge, no explanation. He was right, I wore those out in NYC.

Next up, again while I am on the phone, a guy comes in and smiles at me and then disappears under my desk. In just a moment I can feel that he is shining my shoes. I tell him to stop and that I did not need a shine. He tells me it is a perk of the job and his pay depends on me getting my shoes shined...that it is all paid for and he accepts no tips. Hell of a deal, I got my shoes shined twice a week.

Then there was the guy who would come into the office every so often and give you a shoulder and back rub while you worked or talked on the phone...no charge. The perks went on and on and never stopped and people used company credit cards like gift cards, nothing seemed to be off limits. It was a confusing, interesting, upside down world coming from my sheltered years at Allstate and living in the Midwest.

CHAPTER TWENTY

Donny and Linda Meet Mrs. Doctor Feel Good

I learned about another perk in NYC...magical medical services. I found out about this one when I had a meeting with the big boss and he noticed I was sick as heck. I looked horrible and felt like hell. He asked me what was wrong, and I told him I was coming down with a cold or the flu or something more lethal and I felt terrible. He told me to go home and get some rest. I told him I would love to, but I needed to be on a plane for Seattle, leaving in about three hours, for an important business meeting.

The boss called in his executive assistant and asked her to set me up with a doctor...a very specific doctor. He told me she would see me and fix me up right away and that the company would pay for the whole thing. She worked on the floor of one of the major stock exchanges in NYC...walking distance from our location. I walked over. She saw me immediately. Asked me several questions, checked me over carefully, told me what she thought I had and disappeared for a moment. She came back with two bottles of pills and instructions for their use and told me to roll up my sleeve, she was going to give me a shot. I did and she did, and I was off to the airport.

By the time I got to the airport, I was well. Not better...well. I have never seen anything like it. I did not feel drugged up or numb or buzzed or overly jacked up...I just felt well. She was a miracle worker.

Now, Linda had the same thing I did. So, I asked the doctor if I could send her in. Sure, she said, but the company would not pay for the visit. So, I thought maybe Linda should just go see our regular doctor and avoid some expense. That was before I got treated and healed in about half an hour. Before I got on the plane,

I called Linda and gave her instructions on how to access this doctor. She did so, with much similar results. It took about 30 minutes for me to feel completely cured. Linda took nearly 40 minutes for the full cure. A bit slower, but another damn miracle.

The third miracle came when we got the bill for Linda's appointment...$850 in 1990s money. Ouch!

To this day, I have no idea what was in that shot, but whatever it was, IT WORKED. Never saw that doctor again, but I will never forget her. And Linda and I often speculate what was in the shot...meth...speed...steroids...cocaine...a mixture of all of the above? I'm going to take a wild guess that long-term usage of whatever it was would not be good for you. Only in NYC.

CHAPTER TWENTY-ONE

Getting Ready for Change...
the Transition from NYC to Baltimore

Penn Way was a dream boss. He knew everyone. He understood both the NYC insurance business and how to get things done within our company. He was much like me in that he had no cocaine habit, had no girl friends on the side, did not drink to excess and did not sport a snap-on toupee. We got along great. He was generous in sharing the perks of the job...baseball games, plays, dinners and outings. He had us up to his house a few times in Christmas Cove, Maine, where he had a great wife, wonderful home, an art gallery that his wife ran and a fantastic wooden speed boat. Linda and I loved Penn and he loved us.

One of the heartbreaks of my life is that Penn died early from cancer. Linda had stopped by to see him while she was in Santa Fe, New Mexico, to visit her best friend, Karin. Penn and his wife, Helen, had recently retired to Santa Fe. Linda immediately called me and said that I had better get out there pronto if I wanted to see Penn again...he appeared to be fading fast. There were no flights available for the next day...so I got in my car in Chicago, drove all night and saw him the next day. Thank God I did...he was gone just a short time later. I miss him to this day.

Damn, I loved NYC. I loved going to my cousin's recording studio and seeing big time bands and singers put together their albums. I loved sitting around with him and his wife until sunup talking about anything and everything. Got to admit that I enjoyed seeing celebrities on the streets almost every day, going to CBGB in the East Village with my cousin as he evaluated new bands he might want to sign, sneaking into the Late Show with David Letterman on several occasions (I had figured out a blind spot in their security and had my run of their place...which I used for good and not evil), going to concerts in Central Park or small clubs and seeing shows on or off Broadway. We went to the comedy clubs all the time and always loved the acts.

Side story on comics...we got to see all the great stand-up comics...loved them. About every other comic has one bit where he or she tries to draw in the audience. It basically uses an audience member as a straight man or sets them up for some fun abuse or to be the butt of a joke. Stand-ups are unbelievably quick on the draw with reactions to anything, especially at the early shows when most of them are sober, but what they are really looking for is the expected answer so they can go into their prepared material.

The most common of these is pointing to someone in the audience and saying, "You sir, where are you from?" Normal answer is someplace out of town or New Jersey or Long Island and the stand-up is ready for all of these answers.

We seemed to always get a table right up front, sometimes directly in front of the mike. Dozens of times the comic would come out and eventually pick me out and ask me the question...sometimes three different comics in a row would ask me that same question. My answer was always the same.... "Ahh...I live next door." That one they were not prepared for. I could almost hear the comic saying "jerk" as Linda and I chuckled to ourselves.

Speaking of comedy...one day I was walking through Central Park on my way to give a noon speech at Tavern on the Green. There is always something going on in Central Park...and on that day it appeared they were shooting some kind of commercial. As I got closer, I could see the crew setting up to shoot and the two people who would be in the commercial leaning against a wall talking. One was dressed as Superman. The other was Jerry Seinfeld. As I approached, Jerry turned toward me and I instinctively put out my hand, which he shook. He then said, "And whom do I have the pleasure of meeting?" and I...dressed in my best black suit, gold power tie, Rolex watch blinging and freshly shined shoes said, "I am Serious Suit Man." Jerry barely smiled and said "Yes, I can see that you are, and I have had a lot of trouble with the likes of you." That was it...nothing more said... just a nice little moment in Central Park.

Penn Way III left our company and moved out of town. My cousin became CEO of a record company and moved to Southern California. My friend Bill Smith, who had been right near the top at a rival insurance company in NYC, AIG, moved back to Chicago to become the eventual number one guy at Kemper Insurance. Linda and I were kind of on our own and were liking it less and less. Time for me to move on. In my previous book, *What's Left of Don,* I tell the story about a blind lady and a subway train....it was about then that I decided to leave NYC for a job in Baltimore. And soon, that job was to start the next day...so time for just one more NYC adventure.

The night before I was to start the next morning in Baltimore, my cousin had arranged for a free ticket for me to see my favorite band at the time, in a relatively small setting. The band was Green Day. The setting was the Roseland Ballroom. I attended.

I like things like mosh pits, so I worked my way right up to the front of stage, directly in the middle of the pit. First thing I noticed: I was enveloped in marijuana smoke...not just smelling it...enveloped. Second thing I noticed...this was not a mosh pit, it was a full-on fight...and I was not 21, I was 50. Google "Green Day and Roseland" and see what you find. It was the most violent public event I had ever been in. I was bloody and bruised and saturated with secondhand marijuana smoke. I saw a guy get his leg compound fractured. Green Day even stopped the concert at one point to try to get it back under some control. In other words, I had a fabulous time.

The next morning was not fabulous. I think I got up at 4 a.m., got in my rental car and drove to Baltimore to be there by the opening bell. I met with the CEO and senior staff...some of whom asked me if I was feeling OK...and was sent to HR to fill out papers and the like. Then there was the cup. I had to pee in a cup for a drug test. I asked what they were looking for. First thing mentioned was marijuana usage. I excused myself, found a computer and Googled something like "secondhand marijuana smoke and drug tests." It appeared that it could be a problem.

I have no idea how, but I managed to put off that test for three or four days... and then took it and passed it. That would have been a bitch, to have lost a job for marijuana use when I have never used marijuana in my life.

Linda joined me in Baltimore a few weeks later and then I found out what the term "pent-up demand" meant. We had gone from a big house in Chicago to two different 1500-square-foot apartments...one down the block from the World Trade Center and one at 45 Wall Street in NYC...one for the first year we were there and the other when it first opened for our second year. When we hit Baltimore, Linda set out to get us back into a real home again. It worked. We bought an 8000-square foot home on several manicured acres in a beautiful suburb of Baltimore. We loved it there...and then we got our first winter heating bill. The whole house was heated with electricity. Our monthly bill came to just $3800. Whoops.

CHAPTER TWENTY-TWO

Strange Happenings in Washington, D.C.

Where we lived in Baltimore was about an hour by car from Washington, D.C. I love our capital. So much to see. Let me tell you about a couple of odd experiences we had there...

My parents came to see us in Baltimore. Toward the end of their visit, my dad mentioned that they had never seen Washington, D.C. As you probably know or can guess, D.C. can be a zoo during normal business hours. My folks were in their early 80s. I did not want to put them...or me...through the stress of a visit during the busy hours.

I suggested we go on Sunday, arriving there at 6 a.m. We could park easily, walk around the outside attractions and see virtually everything they wanted to see on foot or by car. They agreed. It worked out perfectly. I made one unusually good decision...two of their favorite people/relatives in the whole world were going to surprise them while they were with me in Baltimore. I had come up with the idea that Dave and Shirley Kahne would hide behind Abe at the Lincoln Memorial. I would walk my folks up there at 7:00 a.m. and surprise them when we walked behind the statue ourselves. Then I thought about the chances of Mom or Dad having a heart attack and how much that might detract from the day...so we surprised them back at home...with no ill consequences.

After we wrapped up our whirlwind tour of D.C., it was still only about 8:00 a.m. Dad had one more request--he wanted to see the Smithsonian's National Air & Space Museum. Off we went.

Dad had spent his post-Army career in the aerospace industry. He worked on the F86, F100, X-15, B70, B1, B2 stealth bomber and more. Two of the planes he had invested countless hours in hung in the Smithsonian...the X-15 and something called HIMAT...a one-third size plane that was highly maneuverable, flown like a drone and could deliver an atomic bomb. Dad wanted to see his planes.

I explained that it was 8 a.m. on a Sunday and that the museum was closed. Dad did not care, he wanted to see his planes. So I drove up to the entrance, had them get out of the car and stand side-by-side looking as pitiful and old as possible and I went over to talk to the National Park Service guard who was on duty. I explained that my dad and mom were in their last years, that they were leaving for home in California in a few hours, that they would never be back, that Dad had served long years in the Army and came ashore at Normandy and had been on the teams that built several of the planes and the capsule for our moon lander... and that he desperately wanted to see them right now. She explained that would be impossible and that I needed to leave immediately. She also mentioned that she was concerned someone might sneak in because the door to the museum was open and she had to go around to the other side of the building for exactly 15 minutes to take a break.

I could not believe my ears. The guard walked off, I ushered my parents in, we saw all the planes and more and got back outside to assure the guard that nothing had happened while she was gone. And, I might say, that chunk of moon rock looks great right here in my office.

Second up is a story about the dedication of the Korean War Veterans Memorial in Washington, D.C. On July 27, 1995, I was on my way to work in Chicago and was listening to a National Public Radio segment on that day's upcoming dedication of the memorial in D.C. President Clinton was to do the honors. Linda's dad, Ben Levy, had been killed in the Korean War when Linda was about two years old. All those thoughts went rushing through my head and I drove right past work to the airport, got on a plane and flew to Washington. I have never done anything like that in my life, before or since. I am not a spur-of-the-moment guy.

I missed the ceremony but not the celebration. The area was hot. It was crowded. I was alone. All of a sudden a poem came into my head. I sat down and wrote it out. Someone asked me what I was writing, and I showed him. He choked up and asked if I would read it to his small group. This repeated itself over and over until I had read it to hundreds of people, many of whom got choked up. I was finally forced off of the memorial by a violent lightning storm...and realized I had no place to stay.

I found a hotel nearby and checked in. I was now alone in Washington, D.C. after an emotional day that was somewhat confusing to me. I was not sure why I was even there. I have never felt so lonely. I thought about who I knew in the area that I might call or go see. And then a long-ago conversation rang loud in my head.

I had an old mentor and supervisor at Allstate in Santa Ana named Clark Moore. Clark was old-school, but a great guy. Somehow we were talking about an upcoming trip for me to D.C. He said, "Better you than me." He did not like D.C. at all. He did say, however, that he would absolutely go there if they were to ever erect a memorial to honor soldiers who served in the Korean War.... that he would be there for the opening.

Now, this had to be 10 to 15 years after that conversation. I got to thinking about it. Clark did not say things lightly...he meant what he said. So, I wondered... if I were Clark and had come to D.C., where would I stay? I concluded that he was not much of a world traveler these days, had pretty simple tastes, was a bit frugal and would want to be as close as possible to the memorial site to make getting there easy. So, I picked up the phone and called the Holiday Inn nearest to the memorial. I asked to speak to Clark Moore. They put me right through.

Clark answered the phone and I said, "Clark, this is Don Hurzeler. I just wanted to call and tell you from the bottom of my heart...thank you for your service in Korea." There was a very long silence. When he finally spoke, he said, "Don, how in the world did you find me? Absolutely no one knows that we are here." I told him that I always kept an eye on him, that I had remembered our long-ago conversation and that I was not going to let this day pass without reaching out to him. I could not tell for sure, but I think I choked up crusty old Clark Moore.

I am proud of those in my family...and my friends...and my fellow citizens who have served in our armed forces. I am so happy I skipped work that day to a have a chance to honor a few of them in person and by phone.

And then there was this D.C. experience that was a delightful surprise...

I got a call from Mercedes Benz. They told me that they appreciated me as a customer and would like to send a perk my way. My guard went up like an electric window in a car...this sounded like a sales pitch to me.

They had noted that I owned two Mercedes...and had owned several prior. Correct. They noted that I lived within an hour of D.C.... also correct. They wondered if I would like to attend a private party at the beautiful Washington, D.C. National Gallery of Art where we would enjoy valet parking, cocktails, a gourmet dinner, a fashion show and an evening of music by Ray Charles and his orchestra. There would be no more than 100 of us there. The only thing remotely looking like advertising would be the new E550 that they would be debuting...just the car off in a separate area, no sales talk, didn't even have to go over to look at it...and they guaranteed there would be no follow-up sales call. This was strictly a thank-you perk for a loyal customer.

We attended. It was exactly what they had promised. Each part of the evening was perfect. Ray Charles could not have been better, and he was just a couple of feet away from my seat. An absolutely fantastic evening. And, yes, I bought the E550...turned out to be the best car I ever owned.

CHAPTER TWENTY-THREE

Dad to the Rescue

I mentioned that I might jump around a bit in this book...well, here comes one of those jumps...back to our time in Chicago.

When my daughter, Stephanie, was about 13 years old, she invited several of her best friends for a sleepover at our house in Barrington, Illinois. I have to say that they were pretty well-behaved, at least I could not really hear what they were doing several doors away on the second floor of our home. Quiet enough that my wife, Linda, and I could actually get some sleep.

I think I fell asleep about midnight...dead asleep. Linda must have fallen asleep about the same time. Lights out, door closed...done for the night.

About 1 a.m. I was startled awake by Stephanie and her friends shaking me and yelling that there were two scary-looking guys trying to climb up to the second story to break into our house. I did not ask for details...I was on it! I ran past the kids, down the stairs, threw open the front door without turning off the burglar alarm and caught the two guys red-handed. They had a ladder and were getting ready to climb right up to my daughter's bedroom. These were not local kids who might be wanting to join the girls for a party; these two guys were hoodlum-looking burglars up to no good whatsoever.

We had a big circular driveway at the front of the house. The door was near the middle of the driveway arc. To the right, the two guys, their ladder and their car. I charged them like a bull in an arena...with my yelling and the burglar alarm adding to the chaos. The bad guys abandoned ship immediately and fled to their car. They managed to get in on both sides of the front seat at just about the time

I got to the car. I flung myself through the air and grabbed onto their windshield wipers and continued yelling at them as loud as I could. I pounded hard on the windshield, trying to break it so I could grab one of them and begin the beating I richly wanted to provide for him. I can still see their faces...just inches away...wide-eyed and terrified.

They threw the car into gear and floored it, with me now hanging on for dear life. I had broken off one of the windshield wipers and was trying to get a grip on whatever was left of it with my right hand. My left hand had a death grip on the other wiper. We were now building up speed and I had a passing thought that maybe I should find a way off of the speeding vehicle. Too late...the way off found me.

At the end of our circular driveway...lurking in the dark...were the two dump truck loads of fresh dirt and mulch that I had had delivered earlier. It was going to be used in our garden the next day because it had been delivered too late to get the job done that day. It stood there like a good-sized, dark hill completely filling the driveway from side to side. The bad guy driving was so busy looking at me just inches from his face that he never saw the dirt pile. He probably hit it going 20 miles per hour...and that brought him to an immediate stop. Not so much me. The encounter launched me...backwards. Fortunately, it was fresh dirt and I hit it flat on my back, so it did nothing more than knock the wind out of me.

The bad guys put their banged-up, no-windshield-wiper vehicle into reverse and dragged some broken part of the car along the driveway as they went. They then turned the car onto my lawn and peeled out to the road. I lay there with one windshield wiper in my hand and surveyed my situation. The bad guys were gone. I was not hurt. And, I realized quickly, the legend of Stephanie's dad and the bad guys would be told for years to come...I had achieved superhero status for sure.

Except...except for one minor detail. Let's call it the tighty-whitie detail. When my daughter and her friends woke me up, I had gone into action so quickly that I had not realized that all I had on were my tighty-whities...my underwear. No tee shirt. No pajamas. Just my white, for the most part, underwear. And did I mention...I was standing right next to Stephanie's best 13-year-old female friends. Oh, the humiliation.

The police caught the would-be crooks. It was not hard to spot a beat-up old car missing a windshield wiper and trailing a major amount of dirt from its smashed-in front end. And I swear this is true...the police told me that the bad guys said they would rather be caught by them than to have to fight with the madman in his underwear who tore up their car. That was a proud moment.

My daughter is almost over the embarrassment of that night. I say almost because it has only been about 30 years since this happened and she figures it will completely fade from memory in another 30 or so. And yes...I was a legend...Mr. Tighty-Whitie, as I was known to her friends.

CHAPTER TWENTY-FOUR

How to Die Quietly at Sea

Jumping around again to get at a story that has been resting in my closet for way too long...

Back when I was in my 30s and 40s, I used to go on long-range fishing trips, often with my father-in-law, Bill Collins, or my dad, Jim Hurzeler, or both. We would leave out of San Diego on a 105-foot boat called the Polaris 105 and go chase tuna. What made it even more fun was that we would stop around the Coronado Islands to catch squid for bait and maybe also a yellowtail, one of my favorite fish to land and eat. Sometimes on these four- to seven-day trips, we would stop in a Mexican port and trade fish for lobsters...and enjoy a feast. Lots of beer aboard, enough to keep you going all day and all night. Quite a trip.

I won't mention the one albacore trip that Bill and Dad and I took...an expensive six-day trip WAY out to sea. Might have been 20 of us aboard. Spent six days without seeing land and, unfortunately, six days at sea without seeing a single fish. We had to stop at a fish market on the way home to buy enough fish to convince the wives that we had spent our time and money wisely.

So, one night on another trip we got into very rough seas. I love rough seas. We were bouncing around in our bunks like ping pong balls, but most everyone had enough booze in them to stay asleep. Apparently I should have had a night cap...I was wide awake.

I got up quietly from my bunk, weaved my way through the sleeping area so as not to wake anyone and went up on deck. What a ride...up the crest of a wave and down the back...repeat. As a lifelong surfer, I loved it.

I made my way up to the bow of the boat so I could maybe see what was coming in the dark. Could not see shit. So I was caught completely flat-footed and not hanging on when we dipped down one wave and ran the bow into a giant swell that was headed right at us. It rocked the boat. A ton of water came over the bow. The water picked me up and swept me 105 feet to the stern of the boat where I managed to catch hold of just about the last solid thing along the way, a handle to the fish gate near the stern of the boat. I let the rest of the wave pass over me, got up and ran for shelter.

No one saw this happen. No one knew I was there. There were not cameras everywhere in those days. Had I gone over the side or off the back in heavy seas in the middle of the night several hundred miles off someplace in Mexico, I'm thinking it would not have gone well for me.

I dried off as best I could and got back into bed, careful to not wake anyone. I got very little sleep that night...kept imagining my dad and father-in-law in the morning saying, "Anyone seen Donny?" That would have been a bad day for all involved...and not a real good day for me. Never mentioned it until now...felt pretty foolish about it and still do.

The next morning, we were greeted by great weather and still rough seas. And we found the tuna. The best place to be for the tuna was the stern of the boat. Everybody wanted to be there. By the time we got our gear together, every spot was taken. Big Bill Collins had an idea. He went over to the bait tank, grabbed about half a dozen live anchovies and put them half in his mouth, biting down gently on them so they could not wiggle away. He then got the attention of a couple of guys on the rail...guys looking a little the worse for wear from the motion of the ocean... and as soon as he got their attention, he sucked in the anchovies and chewed them up and swallowed them. That created a space on the rail for the three of us...the people who witnessed that act were busy puking over the side. Bill was a tough son of a gun.

CHAPTER TWENTY-FIVE

Bill Collins, Malibu, Mayhem and the Mob

Like me in many of these stories, Bill at one time could put away the booze. Except Bill was so large...think center on the football team...that he could do things I had never seen done. Like drink an entire CASE of beer.

The Collins family had a non-fancy house in a very fancy area...Malibu...in the area above Zuma Beach. They shared a driveway and stairs to their private beach with an old actor named Raymond Burr...a heck of a nice guy, but a little quirky. Mr. Burr had a 10,000-square-foot house in front of ours that sat on the side of the cliff overlooking the Pacific. It was 10,000 square feet...with one bedroom. Hell of a bedroom, though. Oh, and he had a small zoo...doesn't everyone?

The stairs to the beach were legendary...hundreds of steps down...and seemed to be way more on the hike back up. First time I went down those stairs on my first trip to the Malibu house, I opened the gate at the bottom to step out onto the sand and a quite famous actress was lying there nude...alongside her equally nude 20-year-old daughter. She stood right up and came over to shake my hand, saying, "You must be Linda's new boyfriend. Her aunt told me all about you." I had very little to say.

So, Big Bill and I and often Bill's sons, Greg and Billy, would walk down those stairs with all of our fishing gear and a case or two of beer. Two beers for me and the rest for Bill. We would catch one great sea bass after another...and we never wasted them...we ate them for dinner with the family.

About two years after I had joined the family, Bill had this brilliant idea. I worked for a company owned by Sears. As such, I could get Sears stuff at a giant discount. Bill had his eye on a 12-foot fiberglass fishing boat...no motor, just the boat. I arranged to get one at the Santa Ana Sears Outlet Store for not much money. Bill was thrilled. We drove down and somehow strapped that heavy boat to the top of his Camaro...no pads or fancy surfboard racks to protect the car...just lashed it to the top of the car and ran the ropes through the windows and then off we went... onto the freeway at 80 miles an hour, beer in hand, from Santa Ana to Malibu. How it stayed on...I have no idea. Had it come loose, it would a have killed a bunch of people and been a little hard to explain to the police.

Once we got to Malibu, we had the minor problem of getting the boat down those stairs. I think we rounded up everyone we could and just hauled it down there holding it over our heads. One way or the other, it made it to the beach.

Now, why did Big Bill want this rowboat on that beach? Because 75 yards out was one of the greatest kelp forests you have ever seen...teeming with great eating fish. The first few times we went out, he would have me go over the side with a swim mask on and scout out the best kelp patch with plenty of fish. I spent most of my time dodging seals and watching for sharks, but I did find the fish...and we had a ball fishing there.

One Saturday, Bill woke up his son Billy...probably nine or ten at the time, and me, and said, "Time to go fishing." We made our way down to the boat. We had a case of beer and Bill had already had several. We rowed out and tied the boat to the kelp...and hauled in fish after fish. Soon, the bottom of the boat was filled with empty beer cans and flopping fish. That was about all I could see...because the famous California fog had rolled in. You had to listen to the wave action to figure out which way the beach was, and Bill and I were both pretty screwed up by now. Young Billy was in good shape and asked me why the waves sounded so loud. I immediately guessed why they sounded so loud...the surf had come up and the tide had changed. Lots of rocks on that beach. Uh-oh.

Time to head to the beach and I suspected this was not going to be pretty. Bill was not in any shape to be making any decisions. I was in much better shape and scared to death, so I took charge. When I could see the waves were getting steep... indicating we were about in the impact zone where those waves would be breaking. I estimated the waves were maybe 10 feet tall...big deadly waves. I commanded Billy to abandon ship and swim to the beach. I was hoping he could get his feet on the bottom, then I could toss him the bow rope and he could pull us in. Yeah... that did not happen.

Billy somehow made it safely to shore...I could hear him, but not see him. Then, out of the fog bank a 10-foot wave appeared directly behind us...and it started to break. I dove hard at the bottom of that wave and passed right under it.

Bill was enjoying a beer on board at the time and got quite a surprise. The wave picked up the boat, threw Bill and everything into the sea and then just plain beat the hell out of him. I had to swim through the debris field of beer cans, expensive fishing gear and fish in varying degrees of dying to finally grab Bill and drag him up onto the sand. We spent the next hour trying to clean up the beach and salvage gear...which turned out to mean, "See if any of the cans are still full." Amazingly, no injuries, but that was the last voyage of my Sears 12-foot fiberglass fishing boat. It may still be there somewhere on the beach.

Another day the fishing was the best I have ever seen. It was just Bill and me and we were catching one fish after another from the beach. After a while, I noticed that the first case of beer was gone, and a dent had been made in the second case. I also noticed that Big Bill was having just a bit of problem casting. His timing seemed to be off for some reason.

Before long I heard a snapping sound. Bill had managed to catch the fishing pole between two rocks and then accidentally broke it in two trying to get it out. I went over to see if I could help. Only coffee could have been of some help at that point. Big Bill was in bad shape. I suggested we call it a day.

No way. Bill was not about to leave when the fishing was this good and some of the beer was still cold. He said he would fix it. How he fixed it was he broke all of the fishing rod off with the exception of the handle that held the reel and line. He then got a huge fishing hook...one about the size of your finger if you were to bend it into a fishhook shape. He rigged up nearly a pound of lead weights. You need some weight...not that much weight...to whip out as you cast the hook, line and sinker.

On the giant hook he placed a giant piece of squid. I am not sure what he was going for, but I doubt a bass could even swallow this piece of bait. He then did the only smart thing he had done in an hour or so...he told me to stand back...and I did.

Bill swirled this pound of weights, giant hook and a couple yards of fishing line around his head like a cowboy at a rodeo. Around and around it went. By the time he let it go it was moving so fast you could hardly see it. Wham...he let it go. Next thing I know, Big Bill is down on the sand and cussing. I walk over to see what is wrong and plenty was wrong. He had let go at the wrong time (big surprise) and that hook had gone into the palm of his hand on one side and came out the other...with a small piece of squid still on it. Squid and hook on one side of the hand and squid and hook on the other. After he got done cussing and showing me the disgusting-looking hand, he said, and I quote..."I'll bet that hurts."

There were no cell phones in those days and apparently the naked actress and her daughter had the day off, so there was no one around to help. Just me and a bunch of fishing gear and empty beer cans and Bill with a hook through his hand... and hundreds of steps ahead of us.

I got behind Bill and dragged along as much stuff as I could and kept an eye out in case he staggered backwards and crushed me like a bug as he careened down the stairs and fell back to the beach. Much to my amazement, we made it up the stairs to the house. At the house he grabbed two beers for the road, and I drove him to an emergency room in Malibu...fishhook and squid still embedded in his hand. It was a quiet ride. He did, however, insist that I stop at Trancas Market to re-supply the beer.

At the emergency room, Big Bill, now completely hammered on pain and beer, was ushered into an examining room. The doctor looked over his disgusting-looking hand and shook his head. Bill then asked him the one question that I think any of us would ask at that point..."Doc...do you think I will need a vasectomy?"

I promise you that is exactly what he said. The doctor about fell out laughing and said that he would not need a vasectomy but that he might need a few cups of coffee. He then cut the pointy end of the hook off, removed as much of the squid as he could and pulled the hook out. He cleaned the wound and asked Bill if he wanted it stitched closed or if he would rather leave the hole open so he could use it as a whistle. Wrong question...Bill immediately put the wound up to his mouth and blew as hard as he could...and there was sound, but not really a whistle. It was the sound of the doctor being annoyed because he now had to clean the wound again...and put a bandage on it this time.

Bill liked everyone. He liked to talk with everyone. He liked to listen to everyone. If you had stories to tell, Bill was going to be your friend. Examples...he talked to a bartender in Israel so much while on numerous business trips there that he ended up sponsoring the guy's move to the U.S. and he was frequent visitor at the house in Malibu.

Bill met a guy on a plane ride from the East Coast to Los Angeles. Chatted him up. Loved the guy. Next thing you know, the guy gets invited to stay with us up at Malibu. And...he accepts.

Linda and I go up to Malibu for the weekend and here is the guy...he and Bill are headed to the beach to go fishing. I talk to the guy a bit and my "I don't like this guy at all" alarm goes off. I kind of quiz him. They head off fishing. I head to the phone to do some checking.

Perfectly sober, extra friendly, Big Bill has brought this total stranger up to stay with us at Malibu for an undetermined length of time. I track down who this guy is. He is an East Coast mobster whose brother was murdered in a vicious mob hit two days ago. He and his brother were partners in their "waste management" business. Let's guess why this guy was on a plane to the to the other side of the United States and eager to accept the kind offer of a place to stay in a remote area of Malibu. There were people out there right then trying to find him and kill him... and he was with us!

I faked a bleeding ulcer attack to get us out of the mess and to get the guy out of the house. And for weeks, we were reminded of his visit because his photo would be on the evening national news along with the story as to how he had now gone missing. Oh Bill.

OK...I was just reminded of two more Big Bill stories...

Bill and Alice, Linda's mother, came to see us when we were living in Pittsburgh. It was the coldest week in recorded history in Pittsburgh. Not the kind of weather that would impress two Californians who had flown in for a visit.

The first moment of off-putting cold weather happenings came as Alice screamed, "Look at that man!" We were driving through an area known as Bridgeville and some old guy was out trying to get the ice off of the sidewalk. He had apparently been working hard for quite a while as he had a six-inch nose icicle...a piece of ice hanging down from the end of his nose. You just don't see that very often in Southern California.

Next up, I took Bill with me to try to wash my filthy car before I gave them the guided tour of Pittsburgh...which, when not frozen solid, is one of the most beautiful cities in America. Drove all around town looking for a car wash that was open. That should have been a good hint...but it was not. I finally found a coin-op car wash place open.

I left Big Bill in the car with the motor running because, although it was a bright blue sunny day, the temperature was minus three and the wind was howling. I was afraid to turn off the car.

I put in my money and fired up the wand used to spray off the car...had it set to the soap cycle. Happy to say it worked, but the soapy water instantly turned to a sheet of ice as it hit the car. It was as if I was painting the car in thick, soapy ice. I covered the entire car before I noticed it was actually getting lower and the tires were bulging from all the weight I had just painted onto it.

I stopped what I was doing and surveyed the situation. Nothing to do but quit, get in the car and drive out of there...hoping that each pothole along the way would knock off some of the ice. I could not see inside the vehicle due to the soap ice coating on the windows, but I could hear Big Bill laughing inside the car. I then tried to get in the car. That was a no-go...I had sealed the car tight with ice.

Took me many long minutes to beat the ice off of the doors and out of the locks and many more long minutes to clean the ice off the windshield with the only thing I had for that chore...all of my credit cards. These efforts turned out to be the highlight of the whole trip for Big Bill...he loved it.

But life has a funny way of evening things up...and karma can be a bitch.

Big Bill did not get his name from being tiny...he was a big boy. He was a big boy because he loved to drink and eat. He did both most of the time. And Pittsburgh was the perfect place for that...it has plenty of local beers and some of the great restaurants in the world, like my favorite, Tambellini's.

So one night I arrange for us to all go to Tambellini's. This would be an expensive night and there would be more food put in front of us than an army could consume. I explained this to Big Bill...but apparently that was not good enough for him. I had just bought an entire case of packaged treats and when I came in to talk to him and tell him the ladies would be ready to go in another ten minutes, I found the wrappers for my new bag of goodies strewn all around the floor...he had all but finished off my expensive bag of individually-wrapped treats all by himself...BEFORE we were to head off for a feast. I was pissed, but my salvation was right there at hand.

I asked Big Bill how he liked the treats. He said he loved them, best beef jerky he had ever eaten. I told him Snowflake loved them as well. He asked why I would give any of these to our dog. I told him we give them to him because they are doggy treats that came from a local place that turned road kill into "beef jerky" doggy treats...and handed him one of the labels....which listed deer, cat, sheep and beef anus as ingredients. Bill dry heaved for a half hour...one of the best half hours of my life.

Bill lived, somehow, to a ripe old age and is now gone. I miss the big guy. We had some fun together and often his actions made me feel like the sensible guy in the room.

CHAPTER TWENTY-SIX

Stories from the 'Hood

After Pittsburgh, we moved back to Barrington, Illinois, in 1986. The neighborhood featured big houses and a large lake surrounded by open fields filled with birds and wildlife. But, this was Chicago and Chicago has some interesting people.

One of the biggest houses was right on the lake. It was a beautiful house, with an old rich guy and a young beautiful blond. The old guy drove a red Ferrari. The house had armored shutters on the windows that could all be lowered quickly by an electronic system. There were also small slots in those protective shutters just large enough for a rifle barrel or many rifle barrels. If you read my last book, you know that protection like that was sometimes needed for those who did not earn their livings in the traditional corporate manner but more in the traditional Chicago manner.

This old rich guy liked me. Why? Because I was always jogging in the neighborhood and he could catch up to me in the Ferrari and talk to me as I attempted get some exercise...everyone else hid when they saw him coming. The subject was always the same...how would I like to invest some money with him... paid 10 percent interest A MONTH, you would get all your money back at the end of the year...and you could invest even more at that time if you had enjoyed the arrangement...oh, and no pesky tax papers to worry about, this was a tax-free investment.

Now, a bunch of my Allstate buddies back in Brea, California, fell for this deal one time. They were invited to invest $1000 under those exact same terms. They each got paid every penny of promised interest. They each got paid back every dollar of their original investment. There was no paperwork or paper trail... all cash. Hell of a deal...they repeatedly invited me to participate. I declined.

At the end of one year, the guy had 100% of the people who had invested with him willing to go one more round on this arrangement. The guy running the deal explained that it had become too much work with so many people investing, so he was trimming it back to just those investors who were serious and could invest $25,000 or more...a fortune in the 1970s. People dipped into retirement accounts and some borrowed money to participate. That was the last they ever saw of that dude...completely gone...no paper trail...no ability to go to the police and explain how they had criminally avoided paying taxes the year before...no tax deduction possible on their all-cash "investment"...totally screwed. I remembered that as the old guy in the Ferrari cruised along beside me. Never did take him up on his generous offer.

And then there was an even bigger house built on the lake...maybe 12,000 square feet. The couple who built it moved in on a December 30. On December 31, the neighborhood always had a moving New Year's Eve Party...cocktails at one house, dinner at the next, dessert at a third and the New Year brought in at a fourth...loved our New Year's Eve parties...several of which I attended injured, which you might recall if you read my last book.

The young couple...he was 22 and she was 21...were invited and we were all excited to meet them and learn how they could afford such hefty house payments at such a young age. Shortly after they arrived at the party and got introduced around, one of our neighbors proposed a toast to the couple with the highest house payment in the neighborhood. The young guy said, "That would not be us...we paid cash...I earned enough on my first day at work as a commodity dealer to pay cash for the house." They never became the most popular couple in the neighborhood. In fact, the thing you heard most about them was...if you were planning a party and their name came up for an invite you would immediately hear..."Fuck 'em." Guess the rest of us who had regular jobs found it a bit hard to relate to that kind of success.

We had another interesting couple down the street. This was a NICE neighborhood and nice street. The guy was not so interesting. However, the lady, mom of two, was kind of interesting. She became a paid escort and advertised with her photo in various local publications. You would see the limo pick her up and drop her off...and wonder what in the hell the dinner conversation was like at their house.

Two houses past her, a really successful guy of about 60 and his trophy wife of about 30...a blond bombshell. I knew him well. I barely knew her. However, my son and I went out to Phoenix to watch Michael Jordan during his minor league baseball career and we ended up in a casino quite late at night. I looked a couple tables over and there was the blond bombshell...with our local golf pro, a well-known sleazebag. She saw that I saw her and waited until my son walked away, then came over to me. "Is this going to be a problem?" she asked. "Why, yes it is." I replied. She walked away.

The next Monday I got a call from her husband. He called to thank me. Told me that she had come home and admitted everything and mentioned me and that he had thrown her out and was divorcing her. I told him that he had saved my day from being horrible because that note I had sent him about meeting for lunch was to tell him the story. He said he knew...and he appreciated it.

It was the most memorable block I have ever lived on. We loved our next door neighbors, but I drove them nuts. He was an orthodontist and kind of a perfectionist. I am not. He would mow his huge lawn in an orderly manner. I took the speed governor off of my Sears riding mower and would literally get it to go up on two wheels on the turns. I rode that thing so hard that I would often feel it lurch to a halt and look back to see parts and oil behind me on the grass. I had it on a Sears lifetime maintenance agreement with no deductible and they had to repair that bad boy over and over. I would take off the governor and drive it until the oil in the engine turned to a solid...pretty much blow it up and then call them to come get it. Hard to believe, but the head of the Sears Service Center called me and told me I could go to the local store and pick any riding mower they had...brand new... and they would give it to me in exchange for my beater...as long as I did not buy the maintenance agreement on the new mower. Too good a deal to pass up, so I did it... and regretted it. I did not treat the new mower well either. In fact, my orthodontist neighbor would run out of his garage to tell me it was smoking behind me...I think he was afraid I might start a prairie fire.

His wife is one of our best friends also...to this day. However, she is a bit shy and conservative and I think I have always scared her half to death. She made the mistake of giving me the keys to the house in case anything went wrong while they were on a two-week vacation. When they returned, she asked me if all went well. I told it all went spectacularly and that I had enjoyed my tour of her underwear drawer. We were never asked to watch that house again.

Every house had a story...the house where Steve lived...a kid with cerebral palsy...a kid I love and loved with all my heart. He had kind of an adult trike and would follow me around the neighborhood when I was not being pestered by the old guy in the Ferrari. He had my back in case any cars came along...he would pull out his toy guns and wave them around. I loved our runs...Steve was and is my buddy.

CHAPTER TWENTY-SEVEN

Walk In Like You Own the Place

Jumping around again...here we go.

I have found in life that if you act like you belong there, security will hold the doors open for your entry. I have tested the limits of that idea countless times.

My son and I went to the NBA All-Star Game in Chicago on a cold February night in 1988. We went to the first night, which featured the Slam Dunk Contest won by Michael Jordan, and then to the game itself. Quite a thrill and big thanks to our friend Bryan McTernan for the tickets.

The first night we got there just as the NBA West All-Stars arrived by bus. Kareem stepped off the bus, then Magic, and then I stepped in behind Magic and then Coach Pat Riley and then my 14-year-old son, Jim, and then the rest of the team. Jimmy and I just kept walking like we were part of the team. We walked right through the arena door without anyone asking for our tickets. When we got to the door of the locker room. I walked right in. A cop grabbed Jimmy. I didn't bother to notice. I was now in the locker room with the entire NBA West All-Star team. There was no one else there...no press...no security...a suit or two who were probably League officials...and me. I talked with several of the guys...no one ever asked what the hell I was doing there. Maybe 20 minutes later, the team and I went onto the arena floor for our shoot-around prior to the game.

I cannot tell you how much fun I was having passing the balls back to the guys taking their shots. This was a dream come true. I did my best to ignore the distant distress calls from my son...until I heard an adult voice also yelling my name. I reluctantly looked up to see the cop holding my son by one ear...and motioning to me to come up into the stands. Heck, I was needed on the floor, I did not have time for those two...but the cop insisted.

I said my goodbyes, wished my team well and headed up to retrieve my son. Well, turns out Jimmy was a bit upset with me. I had both tickets...he had none and no one believed his story that his dad was with the All-Stars until Jimmy was actually able to point me out (or as I thought of it...rat me out) to the cops. They had threatened to put him out into the sub-freezing cold in an area not widely known for welcoming wandering around freezing youngsters at night. I produced our two tickets and Jimmy and I headed for our great seats...not as good as being on the court, but nice seats nonetheless.

I have walked backstage at the Hollywood Bowl to meet the musicians after several shows...no one ever tried to stop me. Did the same at Carnegie Hall the first time we went. Linda said she looked up after the show to see me directly behind that evening's star on my way back to his dressing room for a drink...he never asked me what I was doing there. In my last book I told the story of my being in the ring for the main event of a WWF wrestling match...uninvited and in front of 16,000 people. And then there was the time I took Ted Turner's seat directly next to the bench at an Atlanta Hawks game...and I snuck into an event to shake hands with President Bush...in fact I did that with both of the Bush presidents.

But my best sneak-in BY FAR was the night that Cal Ripken Jr. broke Lou Gehrig's record for consecutive games played—2131 games in a row...amazing. I am a baseball nut. This was a once-in-a-lifetime chance. I flew from Chicago to Baltimore for the game. I had $1000 cash in my pocket to pay the scalper. The scalpers laughed at me...tickets were going for $3000 and more. I tried everything... nothing worked. I then cased the stadium to look for the weak point where I might sneak in...and found it. It was a high and sharp fence that was not well lit. I was still in my forties and figured I could climb it and jump down inside the stadium. A young guy showed me the way. When he jumped, he compound fractured his leg...just on the other side of the fence from me. That did not look like much fun. I searched some more.

Pretty soon I ran out of time...I could hear the Star Spangled Banner being played...the game was about to begin, and I was going to miss this historic moment. So, I devised a quick plan...I would get in line with the stragglers (who in their right mind would be late for this game?) and when I reached the ticket taker I would hand him my $1000 wad and see what happened. My heart was pounding as I moved up in line. When I got to him, he stuck his arm out with his hand on my chest and turned to yell at some people trying to rush the line next to him. As soon as that settled down, he motioned me through as if I had already given him my ticket...and I still had the $1000 in my hand. He must have thought he had taken my ticket. I was in.

I knew that I had another immediate problem. There would not be a seat available anywhere. And I also knew that Baltimore did not put up with people wandering around...you would soon get asked for your ticket and then thrown out if you could not produce one. So, another scheme. My theory is that if you have no ticket and need to find a seat, start with the best seats and work your way to the cheap seats. So, I started looking directly behind home plate.

I immediately found a seat on the aisle behind home plate and took it. I had not sat down for more than a moment when I heard a voice say, "Excuse me, that is my seat". I looked over and it was Bruce Hornsby...he had just played the national anthem. I apologized and started to get up when he said, "No...please stay...just act as my buffer for anyone wanting an autograph, I really want to watch this game." I was on it...he did not have to sign anything all night and I had one of the best seats in the house.

At one point I heard a familiar voice right behind me...someone I had met once before...a hero of mine...Joe DiMaggio. Mr. DiMaggio was preparing to go on the field to honor Cal Ripken Jr....and I will never forget his opening words to Cal..."On behalf of my teammate, Lou Gehrig..." Can you imagine?

President Clinton and Chelsea and Vice President Gore and his then wife, Tipper, all stopped by to say "hi" to Bruce Hornsby...reaching across me as if I did not belong there...how dare they? It was a magical night...and one I mentioned about a thousand times when I moved to Baltimore to work there. I learned quickly that every person who had ever lived in Baltimore now claims to have been at that game...so no one ever believes my story...but it is entirely and completely true.

A bit more about Cal Ripken Jr. The guy is a total stud...big, tall and good-looking. Linda and I ended up spending quite a bit of time in his company. We even thought seriously about buying a house he was vacating. We were the first to look at it...literally as the moving truck pulled through the gates and left. Linda and the real estate agent went one way and I went another...it was a large property and cheap by the downtown NYC standards where we were currently living. I went into the master bedroom and then into a huge closet...and in the back of the closet I could see a safe. The safe looked like the door was not closed, so I went over to inspect it. Inside was a big bag of money.... a big money bag with the Baltimore Orioles logo on it.

Now, I don't know about you, but when I move I always take my big bags of money with me. Not Cal. I carried the bag into the living room and waited for Linda and the agent. Explained what I had found and gave it to the real estate agent to return to Cal.

Years late, I hired Cal to speak at a business event and Linda and I had breakfast with him. I told him I was the guy who had found the bag of money that was returned to him. He knew what bag of money I was talking about...he had several of the old-time vendors at the stadium collect the old coins they got in change and he would then pay them for those coins...so these were Indian head pennies, real silver half dollars and the like...and a big enough bag of them to be quite valuable. He told me he had no idea what had happened to the bag and he had never gotten it back. I called the real estate agent...and I think he got it back.

Which reminds me of another baseball story...this one, off-season. I was a young kid who had just started working at Allstate Insurance in Santa Ana, California. I had been there maybe two years when the Home Office (the guys with serious suits) came out to audit our office. I was put in charge of transportation for the main guy, Don Shanks...a guy so high up in the organization that I could not even relate to his success. I was put in charge of his transportation, I figured out years later, because that meant getting him early in the morning and driving him back to his hotel after work when everyone else just wanted to go home. Since I was the low man on the totem pole, I got the job. But, I loved it. My first chance to get to know a super star in the company.

One evening, Mr. Shanks asked me if I knew anywhere that sold Anaheim Angels baseball items... he wanted to get some for his sons. I told him I did not, but that I had met the owner of the Angels and I might be able to get us in to see him...not a promise, but worth a try. So next day, Mr. Shanks and I drove over to Angel Stadium on our lunch break. It was not baseball season and the stadium was closed. However, I noticed a really nice car in the parking lot in an area that looked like it might be reserved for the owner. So I walked up to the guard at the gate, pointed at the car and said, "I see that Mr. Autry beat us in. Can you please take us to his office, he is expecting us." I'm guessing Don Shanks thought I actually had an appointment to see him...and the guard did as well. He got his assistant to take us directly up to Mr. Autry's office.

I had met Gene Autry one other time, at a sports dinner at Chapman University. In fact, I sat next to him and helped him to his car when he "became exhausted" after quite a bit to drink. I am quite sure he did not remember me at all.

Gene Autry was a famous actor, starred in many Westerns, had a long running TV series and sold over 100 million records. He owned a record label and the Angles and he was a VERY big deal. And here we were, 23 years old, aspiring to move up the ladder worker-bee (that was me) and super-star big boss (that was Don Shanks) being escorted in to see THE MAN. Neither of the Dons could believe it... but we both acted like we belonged there.

Gene greeted us warmly. He came out from behind his big desk and shook our hands. He explained that his assistant was not in and that he had just stopped by to sign a few papers and could not remember why we were meeting. I reminded of our dinner at Chapman University and that he invited me to stop by and say "hi" anytime (a complete lie). He certainly knew Chapman University...just down the street...and he always supported our sports programs. I was quite sure he could not remember that specific evening...so he faked it and said he remembered it well... so good to see me again. We talked for a few minutes and I told him we did not want to keep him...just wanted to pay our respects. He asked if there was anything he could do for us. I said, yes, we would like to purchase a hat or yearbook or something for Mr. Shanks' young sons...big fans. He went over to his phone and made a call. A few moments later, a gentleman shows up and Mr. Autry tells him to take us to the merchandise room and to let us take anything we wanted...no charge. I think he also signed a ball or cap for Mr. Shanks, but cannot really recall if that is fact.

We said our goodbyes to Mr. Autry and headed to the merchandise room. This was the main storage area for everything they sold during the season. It was filled with great items. Happy to report that we both behaved ourselves. I took nothing. I think Don took either a cap for each of his boys or two yearbooks from the previous year. Whatever it was, it was very little. But, we had our prizes and life was good.

Don Shanks and I stayed best of friends from that day forward. He remained my hero throughout the decades of our friendship and he told the above story often. He came to see us shortly before he passed away and we laughed about that day one last time.

And I did build up a minor...very minor...relationship with Mr. Autry. I saw him at Chapman Hall of Fame dinners and elsewhere around town and always thanked him for treating us so well. He got me tickets from time to time and those resulted in my best friend, Mike Fayles, and my wife, Linda, and I getting to see Clyde Wright throw a no-hitter. It also gave me, and a bunch of folks I took from work, a giant thrill. We saw Nolan Ryan throw a no-hitter against the Yankees...

well, almost a no-hitter. With one out and one on first via a questionable error, Reggie Jackson laced a single up the middle and the no-hitter was lost. Angels won on a one-hitter. One of the most exciting games of my life.

Years later, the Angels were in the World Series. When they won game six, I told my son, daughter and son-in-law that I was going to fly out for game seven and they were going to come with me. I had a wonderful connection that got me decent seats and I flew out from Chicago. The Angels won. We all jumped up and down. I said a little prayer for Mr. Autry...he had died almost exactly four years earlier.

I had to rush to the airport to fly the red-eye back to Chicago for a business meeting the next day. So when I left the stadium the celebration was still going on big time, and I was one of the only ones headed to the parking lot. The local Channel Five TV reporters grabbed me and interviewed me about what it was like see the Angels win. I was on for maybe one minute. My sister, who lived nearby, was watching and was quite astounded to see me at the game and on TV...and I had some explaining to do as to why I did not take her with me.

God bless Gene Autry, Don Shanks, and the Angels...every one of them important in my life.

I guess the following story fits here, barely. But let me crowbar it in anyway...

I hear people talk these days about "sexist." Unless you are as old as I am, you have no idea how bad it was "back in the day." Case in point...the Playboy Club.

Playboy magazine was a big deal when I was a kid. There was no internet. If a guy wanted to see a naked or near-naked woman, *Playboy* was at your service. I would love to tell you how woke or advanced I was back then, but the truth is, I was a horny little kid with zero point zero chance of seeing a naked woman in the wild, so *Playboys* got bought. Sorry...but that was the way it was and I was quite happy for the educational experience that magazine provided.

Playboy also had a number of Playboy Clubs that a person could belong to. That was out of my league because it cost real money and I never was able to afford the Playboy Key one needed to go to one of the clubs. I did get to borrow a buddy's key from time to time, so I got to see what went on in those places. Most readers today would be horrified. At the time, some thought the clubs were elegant. Most people today would see them as demeaning and sexist as hell. Young, beautiful women running around in Playboy Bunny skimpy outfits...every one of them hired for their healthy cleavage, which was put on grand display as they were smiling and dipping to serve the men who came in to ogle them, hit on them or otherwise objectify them. I want to tell you it sickened me back then, but it did not. It did, however, ring a few bells of the "this just is not right" kind. Yet, there I was.

On one occasion at the Playboy Club in Los Angeles, my friend and I were waiting for the elevator to open to go up to the club. The doors opened and there was one of Hollywood's biggest stars sprawled out across the floor of the elevator, unable to stand. We got him to his feet and took him over to his car. Instead of resting in the car until he felt better, as he told us he was going to do, he fired that bad boy up and headed home. Quite possibly the drunkest driver ever to make it home alive.

All this leads me to the Playboy Club near Lake Geneva, Wisconsin. I was attending a business meeting/training class at a resort on Lake Geneva. I knew of the Playboy Club nearby. I had a rental car. One night, I invited three or four of my colleagues to go to the club with me. I probably lied to them and told them I was a member...I was not. Again, I had borrowed my buddy's key. I doubt any of them had ever been to a Playboy Club...we were all kind of junior underwriters in the company. They were keen to go.

So we drove to the club. We had dinner and a few drinks...not too many because they were expensive as hell. I excused myself during dinner and found the disco that was one floor down from the dining area. It was early and the only person there was the one Playboy Bunny who was going to be the DJ for the evening. She was a beauty, and in her skimpy Bunny outfit. We talked for a couple of minutes and I told her I was there with my friends. I then said that she could make me an absolute legend if she would put on a slow record and come over to our booth and ask me for a dance. I noted a significant reluctance to participate in my grand plan, but a $20 bill ended that and the deal was made.

A half hour or so goes by and we all drift down to the disco. By now there are people there and the dance floor is crowded. We sat at our little table and watched the scene. We were all married guys and none of us was looking to do anything other than watch what goes on at a Playboy Club. And there was plenty going on.

All of a sudden, the crowd kind of parts and here comes the DJ...who had just put on a slow record. Well, this got our full attention because it looked like she was coming directly over to our table. She did. The guys were in shock. She then pointed to me and said, "Excuse me, sir, I have had my eye on you since the moment you came in, could you please share this dance with me?"

At that, I looked around at each guy,...again, just about stunned at this development, and then back up to her. I said, "Young lady, I would love to, but I am with my friends and I am enjoying their company too much to leave them. Maybe some other time."

Jaws dropped. I had turned down a Playboy Bunny for a slow dance to remain with my friends. Wow!

The Playboy Bunny was much less impressed. I believe the word "pissed" would cover it. I had played her and she did not appreciate it one bit. I never returned to that club again. Probably a wise decision. There may well have been a sign up to watch out for a rude guy from California. That would be me.

Have I ever gotten in trouble sneaking into some place? Glad you asked. I have. The first time I ever did it, I got in trouble. I was really young at the time...maybe six or seven. I had a relative who was in charge of some part of the prison system in California...a favorite "uncle" (actually a second or third cousin). He took me up to meet the governor of California and I got to sit in his chair in his office and talk with him. Governor Earl Warren...later Chief Justice of the Supreme Court. The next day he took us to Folsom Prison for a tour...back then a medieval-looking place you really would not want to be in for an extended stay. We were being escorted around when I got curious about something and wandered off. Next thing you know, I am in the yard with all the real prisoners...who seem quite surprised to see a little boy walking around with them. I wasn't there for long...half of the guards (my fellow prisoners and I called them the screws) showed up and hustled me out of there. Everyone seemed much more excited about my side adventure than I did. Gave me and Johnny Cash something in common...and the train just keeps on rolling on down to San Antone...you may have to look up that reference.

Nope...hate to admit it...and I am sure many of you consider these trespasses to be a real asshole move...but they have gotten me to places I could never have gotten into any other way, and I do not regret them. I never abused the situation... never stole anything. Got me into the Hermitage Theater in St. Petersburg, Russia to listen in on a rehearsal, and backstage at the Late Show with David Letterman. Linda and I snuck into Tivoli Gardens in Copenhagen to photograph stuff in the hours before the gates opened. I got to sit in the co-pilot's seat of a 737 while flying down the Baja Peninsula to Cabo San Lucas. Got to drive a Shelby Cobra when it was a brand-new car because my dad and I asked Carrol Shelby if we could...and he said yes. Was recently on the field at the Rose Bowl game. Lots and lots of fun... and never got in anyone's way or caused a scene.

CHAPTER TWENTY-EIGHT

The Doo Dah Parade

Yet another jump, but a good one...I promise.

In 1980 or so, I took the family to a parade. The kids were maybe six and four. We were the then (before America woke up to realize that America was made up of all kinds of races and family situations) All-American family...blond mom, fit dad and two good-looking kids, a boy and a girl. Little did my wife and kids know what was just ahead.

When we arrived in downtown Pasadena, California, at the parade route, I disappeared for a while. When I returned, I was wearing a wig, makeup, tights, a tutu and running shoes. When I walked over to rejoin my family, they seemed bewildered.

I then asked one of my friends, a creepy-looking clown on a creepy-looking bike, to come over and entertain my kids before the parade started. He got way too close to them and asked them a bunch of creepy questions and his breath smelled like scotch right out of the bottle. He offered to make the somewhat frightened children balloon animals...asked them what their favorite animals were. My daughter wanted a cat...so he made her a cat and it was cute as could be. My son wanted a teddy bear and a few balloon twists later the drunken creepy clown had made a beautiful balloon teddy bear. This put smiles back on the faces of my kids. As they reached out to claim their balloon prizes, the clown placed the balloon animals under the front wheel of his creepy bike and ran over them...popping both loudly and laughing as he drove off to "delight" another child. They looked up at their dad for sympathy...their dad also now well under the influence of the same bottle of scotch...and got nothing more than a drunken smile. And so, our day began...

This was so many years ago that any names I mention are now long forgotten... and they were only local legends anyway. But it was a star-filled afternoon...maybe 100,000 people lining the exact same route that the Rose Parade had used a week prior...maybe 300 people in various stages of dress and drunkenness actually in the parade...this was the Doo Dah Parade.

Most of Southern California in the 1980s was a laid-back kind of a place. Tee shirts and shorts. Beater cars and Mustangs. Street fairs and outdoor concerts, with lots of weed in the air. Not so much Pasadena. Pasadena was filled with upright citizens. They had the Rose Bowl. They had the Rose Parade. They had a museum or two with actual oil paintings in them, all done without the help of numbers or spray paint. People wore suits...some wore hats...ties were mandatory on the gentlemen...and they were gentlemen. Women wore white and dressed with nice accessories. This was a proper, somewhat snobby town of productive members of our society...too far away from the beach to be corrupted by those of us creatures who lived there. It is right up against the beautiful mountains that overlook Los Angeles. A lovely town with some rich traditions.

There are bars in Pasadena where the above description of the citizenry does not fit. Inside those bars, the sons and daughters of the upright citizens...more into having fun and exploring the counterculture than into vying to be Rose Parade organizers. These were not the traditional troublemakers you may have encountered in bars during your lifetime...these were creative troublemakers with twisted senses of humor...my kind of people.

One of these not-quite-right bar flies was a friend of mine. He invited me to participate in the parade itself and offered to make me an official member of the Queens Court. How could I resist?

The parade directly poked fun at the uptight and perfect Rose Parade. It was an inside joke. That joke has continued 40 some years and the Doo Dah Parade is still held.

I should also mention that I was working for a very serious and somewhat prudish company at the time...and I will not embarrass Allstate by mentioning its name. I was a department manager...kind of a big deal. I had over a hundred quite nice, smart (except for one of them) people working for me in Brea, California. I envisioned myself rising up the ranks to chairman of Allstate and expected that I would then take over the parent company, Sears, Roebuck. I was on my way to the top (at least in my head). I knew I could not be associated with this kind of foolishness and stay on my corporate success quest...thus I dressed up in the tutu and wig and makeup. Who would know?

Now, I know you do not know the name Gypsy Boots, but you should. Gypsy, or Boots as many of us called him, was the first actual wild man I had ever met. He was full of good cheer, fun, energy, happiness, vegetables and showmanship. He had lived in caves, was a hippy before there were hippies, ran a health food store before there were health food stores and would show up anywhere there were people...parades, concerts, athletic events, parties...or TV cameras. He carried a cowbell and rang it all the time. He would talk your ear off, and you would leave wondering what the hell he had just told you. You could not NOT have fun around this guy...he was a traveling, electric, genuine, non-conforming, unique barrel of fun...I loved him. He joined me as the only other male in the Queens Court. One point of distinction for me...I was the one the Queen had chosen to wear the coveted sash that said "Coronate Me." Gypsy and I, and a group of lovely young and not-so-young ladies, led the Doo Dah Parade...leaving my family to fend for themselves.

I cannot possibly express how much fun this was for me. As I said, my kind of people, and I was surrounded by them. In back of me were the Brief Case Precision Marchers...a bunch of normal looking, black suited investment bankers with brief cases performing fairly amazing acts of precision marching and flinging around of the briefcases. Behind them was the official band of the Doo Dah Parade...still the official band to this day...Snotty Scotty and the Hankies. And the list goes on and on. I have attended enough of these events that I tend to mix up the performers from one year with those from another year...but a beginning list would include...

The Nude Beach Beauties...barely dressed, mostly women, a very popular group that helped get the party going with their frequent flashes and their tossing of the traditional tortillas into the crowd.

The Lawn Mower Drill Team...men and women with gas-powered lawn mowers doing intricate routines as they marched together through the streets.

The Nuke the Whales float that featured a whale and a nuclear bomb explosion, indicating the desire to nuke the whales to save our oceans, the water we swim in, from being pooped in by the whales.

A group called The Bastard Sons of Lee Marvin...no idea what they were up to.

The Men of Leisure Synchronized Nap Team...a group I had hoped to one day join.

The Radioactive Chicken Heads...again, no idea.

The Billionaires for Wealthcare...with their slogan of "Save the 1%."

The year I was in the parade there was a float that is kind of hard to forget. It was titled Trickle-Down Theory...a popular economic description by Art Laffer of the economic program under President Ronald Reagan. The float consisted of a fairly real looking Republican donkey, out the ass of which was pushed out a constant supply of jellybeans (President Reagan loved jellybeans) that landed on an actual black guy inside a dumpster behind the donkey. I'm thinking the black family that put this float together and manned it was not entirely convinced that the Trickle-Down Theory was working out well for them.

Dr. Demento was there, playing very odd songs for the crowd. The doctor was a weekly radio host in Los Angeles for decades.

Richard Simmons was there often...looking fairly normal in this group of people.

The Committee for the Right To Bear Arms marched every year I went...a dozen or so old ladies marching down the street, waving mannequin arms at the crowd and flinging yet more tortillas.

Followed by people in bear suits with rifles with the slogan, "The Right to Arm Bears"

One guy was dressed up like President Reagan with his nose in the air and a sign that said, "I smell hippies."

A group called Make Cheese, Not War.

The Little Old Lady from Pasadena who was neither little nor a lady.

Zeke the Sheik, who wore a huge actual cactus on his head for no apparent reason.

The Pink Slipped Teachers of California

Save the Ta-Tas...a group of ladies who demonstrated WHY the ta-tas needed to be saved.

And every creepy-looking clown that ever inhabited your worst dreams.

And me...and the Queen...her court...and Gypsy Boots.

What an amazing day...until...

Halfway through the parade, I was having a ball, waving at the crowd with my best Queen Elizabeth regal wave, posing for photos with people along the way, trying to keep Gypsy from ringing that damn cow bell, putting up with the advances of the various members of the court and the Queen...featuring only those at least 20 years older than I and flinging tortillas to the crowd, as was the tradition. How could life be any better? And then...I heard a very loud voice from the crowd...."Hurzeler"..."Don Hurzeler"..."Don, it's me, Tom Brown."

Tom was a top sales manager for Allstate in Pasadena. He had somehow recognized me. This was BAD. I put my head down, tried to blend in with the "security team" of drunks who were trying to clear the way for us, and then slipped into the crowd to circle back, gather up my somewhat upset and confused family and beat feet to the car. I slept not one moment that night. My career was likely at an end.

The next day, first call of the day at the office, Tom Brown. "Don...you were magnificent." I pretended I had no idea what he was talking about. "Don't give me that shit, that was you...leading the damn Doo Dah Parade...biggest shock of my life." Again...had no idea what he was saying. And then he said..."Damn, I sure wish I had had a camera with me." That gave me a bit of relief...at least he did not have the evidence.

Although my buddy Tom mentioned that day to me a hundred times or more, I never confessed, and he never ratted me out. However, I did feel like I had pushed the limit just a bit too far...and it was my last Doo Dah Parade...at least as a participant.

Today, there are Doo Dah Parades in Pasadena; Columbus, Ohio; Kalamazoo, Michigan; and Ocean City, Maryland. If you ever get a chance, attend...or get a tutu and lead the parade.

CHAPTER TWENTY-NINE

The Macy's Thanksgiving Day Parade in NYC and the Tragic Death of Barney from Sesame Street

Linda and I tried to do all the traditional things in NYC...Times Square on New Year's Eve for the drop of the ball and the frozen vomit everywhere, the fireworks over the Statue of Liberty on the 4th of July, a ticker tape parade when the Yankees won the World Series, the New York City Marathon (which I ran and completed), concerts in Central Park, the Gay Pride Parade, the Puerto Rican Day Parade, the St. Patrick's Day Parade complete with more frozen vomit everywhere, Carnegie Hall, the Roseland Ballroom, ice skating at Rockefeller Center, concerts at Radio City Music Hall, the Staten Island Ferry, Madison Square Garden...you know the list. We only lived in NYC for two years, so we crammed in as much as possible... even took the subway for a day at the beach on Coney Island and rode the roller coaster. Did it all.

One of those traditional events was the Macy's Thanksgiving Day Parade. As luck would have it, the year we attended it was both extremely cold and windy... really windy. This was going to be fun, because the parade features huge blown-up balloon characters that float above the street and are so big they can hardly make it around the corners...characters like Donald Duck and Batman...and Barney from Sesame Street. Barney was enjoying a major run of luck and had become the number one most beloved character for children everywhere. I have no idea why... he was big and purple, and I don't even know what he was supposed to be...maybe a dinosaur of some kind.

So, the street was packed...as everything always is in NYC. Parents, nannies, cops, kids, tourists, pickpockets and frozen vomit with a splash of pumpkin pie everywhere we looked. We had a ringside place to stand...right on the curb, with the characters hovering over us as they went by. And it became quite a show. The wind was having at the characters...big time. A wind gust would catch a floating character and head it toward a light pole and the people trying to hold onto it using ropes would get pulled off their feet and dragged down the street until the gust passed. It became kind of a disaster waiting to happen. Someone actually got very badly injured that year when a character brought down a light pole or some such happening.

Well, everyone oohed and aahed as each character passed. The kids would shout out their names as if Superman was going to turn and say, "Oh, hi, little Jimmy, so glad you could come out today." But, it was cute, and everyone was having a great time. Then...

Barney made the turn and came toward our position. I thought the kids were going to go out of their minds. "Barney...Barney," they shouted at the big plastic bag of air on some strings. This seemed to be literally the biggest thing that had ever happened in these kids' lives.

It was about that time that a huge gust of wind hit Barney and he veered hard to the left. Two of the guys trying to hold him down with the ropes were lifted off the ground. People from the crowd helped them to their feet and tried to add more weight to the ropes...but too late. Barney took a hard turn right and took a lamp post to the eye socket. The blow ripped a huge hole in Barney, and he began to deflate. I guess this situation is all worked out in advance because every cop within two blocks instantly jumped on Barney to help deflate him quickly and get him out of the parade route. It was at this moment that I provided my assistance by using my booming voice to yell over and over again, "OH, MY GOD, THE COPS ARE KILLING BARNEY. THEY ARE BEATING HIM TO DEATH. HOW CAN WE SAVE BARNEY? PLEASE COPS, STOP THE BEATING. LET BARNEY LIVE....OH NO, BARNEY IS DEAD."

Turns out this was an unpopular commentary. The cops did not like it. The kids all started crying and the parents were not happy at all. Perhaps not my best moment in NYC.

Linda and I decided to leave the parade early. It would be hard to top the death of Barney.

God, I love New York.

CHAPTER THIRTY

Passing Time in Traffic

I lived and worked in Southern California up until the time I was about 35 years old. I never had a job "down the street." I always had an "L.A. job," which meant a one-hour (on a good day) drive each way...all of it on the freeway. L.A. traffic will destroy your soul.

My worst commute was from near the beach in Huntington Beach to Brea, California. If you did it at 3 in the morning you might be able to make it in 35 minutes. If you did it at 6:30 a.m., you were in for a one-hour ride. I rarely went to work at 3 a.m.

Back and forth. Back and forth. Same freeway. Same traffic. Same bottlenecks. It would slowly eat you up.

Some of the time I had a rider with me. My friend Tom Zmak and I rode the Brea route for a couple of years...me driving one day and he the next. That helped. We could talk or one of us could do something productive and we saved on gas.

However, most of the time I was on my own. I think you have probably figured out that leaving me alone and bored is a bad combination. And keep in mind, you are not reading about the actions of a 16-year-old kid—virtually all of these things I did on my way to and from my job as a department head of a serious insurance company where I had a great group of people working with and for me...more than a hundred terrific Allstaters and one idiot.

So, I had my bag of tricks. Please remember from my previous book that I am really the only one I am interested in amusing. If something is funny to me...I could care less if others get it or enjoy it...I am a happy camper. That said, many of my routines did amuse the heck out of my fellow trapped freeway drivers...none of whom I knew or would ever meet. I would just put on a very brief show for them and get my reward when I glanced in the rear-view mirror or when they caught up to me to honk their horn or give me a thumbs up or a smile.

Almost all of my routines happened in areas where traffic had come to a grinding halt or we were just plain stuck. My absolute favorite was so simple...I would find a convertible with the top down ahead of me and then slowly pass it with my necktie wrapped around the rear view mirror, my head hanging at a tilt, and my body limp. I, of course, had one eye barely open so I could watch out for traffic ahead, but to the people in the convertible it would look exactly as if I had hung myself. I was REALLY good at this one and it never ever failed to get a howling laugh out of the car next to mine. It is the one and only reason I miss wearing ties today.

My second favorite one was good in slowdowns or in steady traffic. I would do something to get the attention of the driver next to me...a small swerve or I would get too close...it did not take much...most everyone was one inch away from road rage all the time. Once I had their attention, I would roll down my window... road rage style...and stare at them with my sunglasses on...my most serious and challenging look. I could see their blood begin to boil. It was then that I whipped off my sunglasses to reveal the practice golf balls that I had cut in half and shoved in around my eyes. These were all white with holes in them...so I could still see traffic...that kind of looked like huge bulging white eyeballs. These eyes were not what the other driver expected, and they went from "ready to fight" to "laughing out loud" in one moment. Proud of that one.

Another favorite was why my wife would always be missing her stockings. I would steal them and then wait for the right moment...perhaps a stalled car just ahead slowing traffic. I picked a victim and did my "never fail" tricks to get them to look my way. I had pulled the stocking over my head and stretched it tight over my face, making my entire face look like a distorted blob. Crooks used to employ this same technique to rob stores...instead of a mask. Always got a laugh. As you can see, my weapon was surprise...and the fact that my "audience" was both bored to death and probably angry before they encountered me.

I always carried a quart bottle of scotch in my car...a bottle filled with tea. If I saw someone watching me for whatever reason I would start taking big gulps out of the scotch bottle, sometimes finishing a third of it in one pull. I would then wipe my lips and smile. Gave those other drivers something to talk about when they got home.

I also had a big sign that I could put in a side window that said, "HONK HORN IF DRIVER IS ASLEEP...DRIVER HAS NARCOLEPSY." I would roll by pretending to be asleep...and always got a honk. I would then wave or slow down to thank them.

These pieces of stupidity were how I kept sane in the insane world of Southern California traffic. Wouldn't it be wonderful if some old guy picks up this book, reads this section and says, "I'll be darned, I saw that fool on the 605." That would make my day.

CHAPTER THIRTY-ONE

The Reno Sears Store

I'm guessing that this next story will be well received by my male readers and not so well received by my female readers. So ladies, fair warning...the childishness/ sexist/objectification nature of the story is such that it might make your day better if you skipped this chapter and headed on to the next one. I'm not looking to make anyone mad at me...but this might just do it.

When I was young and just starting out at Allstate Insurance, I had a territory that included San Diego, Arizona and Nevada. I figured out later that I had this territory because it required travel from my Santa Ana, California, office to far-flung locations and all of my co-workers were senior to me and did not want to travel. So, I started doing business travel at a very early age.

I loved the travel. The local sales managers would treat us like visiting dignitaries, escort us around the area to meet with the various Allstate Insurance agents and then show us the sights. This gave me a chance to meet new people and to better understand my territory.

A quick explanation of how business was done way back when at Allstate...

Allstate agents were located in offices or in Sears stores. Sears owned Allstate. The agents in the stores had a big booth, usually near the escalators, and one or more agents "manned" the booth. Halfway through the day, there would be a shift change and new agents would come in for the afternoon. I learned early on to time my visits right around shift time so I could catch the agents coming and going.

For reasons I never understood, often the Allstate booth would be right next to the major appliances. All of that explanation is to background a legendary visit I made to the Reno Sears store.

I have a buddy named John Hazelrigg. John was a guy with strong skills in the life insurance sales arena. He and I often traveled together to call on agents. I would pitch our business insurance products that agents could sell to shopkeepers or contractors and he would pitch our life products for individuals or corporate executives. We were a hell of a team—kind of the "A" team when it came to getting agents fired up about our products.

As an aside...John was one of the funniest guys I had ever been around...and still is to this day. He can get me laughing first thing in the morning and keep me laughing all day...always has had that ability. However, he was a dead serious business guy and knew when to flip the switch and get work done. He was a perfect traveling companion.

Case in point...we were both doing presentations in Reno, with me up first, at about 8 a.m. Not sure what got to me...the altitude of nearly 5000 feet in Reno, or maybe a lack of sleep or one too many beers the night before...but whatever, I all but passed out during my presentation. John stepped in and took over without blinking an eye, giving me time to sit down and recover, so I could return later like nothing had happened. To the audience, nothing did happen. But John and I both knew he saved my butt that morning. He was a real pro.

Later that afternoon, John and I are at the A store (the biggest Sears store) in Reno. We are hanging around the Allstate agent booth waiting for the shift change. In comes a showgirl. Let there be no doubt about it...not being sexist here... this was a tall, absolutely gorgeous, provocatively dressed woman who, without a doubt, starred in one of the many shows at the Reno casinos. She was a stunner.

She knew that she had every one of us staring at her...played us like the childish little boys we had turned into when she arrived. She walked right up to me and told me to follow her. All eyes were on us. She marched me over to a washer-dryer in the major appliance section of Sears and asked me about the machine in front of her. I looked around quickly for a salesperson from that section and none was to be found. We were just feet away from John and the sales guys, so I decided to put on a show.

I launched into the best description of the features of that particular machine that you have ever heard. Of course, I was just reading them off the advertising card on the machine, but I sure made it sound as if I were the world's expert on that machine. I pointed out that Sears always sold three levels of major appliances... good, better and best. I assured her that there was only one machine good enough for her...the very best machine Sears had ever offered...and it was on sale today and today only.

I could hear the guys chuckling and I was on a roll. My reputation as a sales guy was growing by the second. Hey, even the beautiful young lady was impressed and she put her arm around me to thank me for going into such great detail for her. This was going super well.

Then I was hit with what I can only say was true inspiration. She had seen enough and I could tell she was ready to make a decision. Two opposing thoughts ran through my head...don't talk past the sale and...give the boys a real show. Since I really did not care about the sale, I chose the latter.

I told her, loud enough for the boys to hear, and winking at them, that she absolutely had to see the excellent construction of these machines before she made a final decision. She said that was not necessary, but I assured her it was indeed necessary. I asked her to take a look at the breakthrough technology Kenmore (Sears proprietary brand for certain appliances) had put inside this dryer. I told her to stick her head in the dryer drum and take a look for herself.

The lady was no dummy. She immediately figured out what I was up to. If she put her head in that washer drum, she would have to bend over in her very short dress and basically flash her beautiful butt at my buddies in the booth. She gave me a look, hesitated, and then went right ahead like I had fooled her into assuming that position. I guess she thought, "Hey, I do this every night for a living, why not make these guys' day?" So, she bent over and placed her head in the dryer.

As she did, she accidentally broke wind...a great big fart that just startled everyone. As you can imagine, she was horrified. She brought her head up out of the dryer and turned her completely red and embarrassed face to me, almost pleading for me to somehow make this right. I chimed right in...I said, "Lady, don't worry about a thing, you are going to shit when you see the price."

No sale was made...but a legend was born. Yes, I am a legend in my own mind.

Hey...try that today and see what happens. Hint...you will be in the unemployment line quicker than you can say, "Excuse me, but before you leave, may I show you our line of air purifiers?"

CHAPTER THIRTY-TWO

The Three-Hat Hustle

I worked in corporate America for over 40 years. I loved it. I worked for and with some of the greatest people I have ever met in my life. Many are lifelong friends. I am so thankful to have had the chance to be on teams with them.

That said, stick around long enough and you will run into an asshole at the office. I am guessing you may have done so in your life. It did not happen frequently to me, but it happened. I do not do well around assholes. They bring out the worst in me and no one really wants the worst in me to come out.

The first odd person I met in the workplace was in no way, shape or form an asshole. In fact, he was a beloved guy and someone I completely respected. I ran into him very early on in my career. He was so high up in the company that he had an office. The rest of us were lined up like cars in a parking lot behind our all-exactly-the-same gray desks...a thousand of them spread over two stories.

This guy I mention was kind of the model for what I wanted to become. I was just out of college with a bachelor's degree in business administration and economics. I was a competitive son of a bitch. I wanted nothing less than to work my way through the chairs to become the CEO of the whole company. I thought that might take a year or two...it took 35.

Looking back, he was a mid-level manager in a regional office, but to my 21-year-old self, he was like a Greek god. Until....

One day I heard a commotion. Something was going on in the Greek god's office...the glass of which you could not see through...no idea what was happening. An ambulance arrived. Pretty soon the Greek god is pushed out of his office and right into the middle of all of us straining to see what was going on. I will never forget it...he had a death grip on his chair so powerful that they could not remove him from it, and he was in a catatonic state that looked like he had just been electrocuted. They had to roll him out of his office in his chair, roll the chair and this poor guy through the entire office and then out front to where the ambulance was parked. When they got to the ambulance, we were all lined up along the huge windows, watching the proceedings. They had to find a way to get him and the chair into the ambulance and secure him so he would not roll around on the way to the hospital. It was a truly pitiful sight.

This shook me up for a couple of reasons. I had never seen what a nervous breakdown looked like...but we were later told that was what he had had. Did not look fun. And...for a young guy watching this...this is what I had to look forward to? Not a great moment for me...or the other guy. In fact, he never returned to work.

A total aside that I just recalled...I was still in college when I started working full time...I had one semester to go. To say that I was low man on the totem pole would hardly cover it. My title was clerk and there was no one lower or newer in the department. I really only got the job because the guy in HR knew me from my track career and was a friend of a friend.

Despite my low status, I had the absolute best view of any of the aforementioned gray desks in the office. I was right next to the window overlooking the quite nice entrance to our building, the orange grove across the street and the Santa Ana Freeway that curved by next to the building. I could not understand how I got this nice little perk. And then one day I noticed an odd-looking hole in the window right next to me. I asked someone what it was and that stirred up some excitement. It was a bullet hole...a brand-new bullet hole. The reason I got that nice desk was that every so often a driver on the Santa Ana Freeway, who was apparently a pretty good shot and had some grievance with Allstate Insurance, would fire off a round at our office...always hitting that same window...my window. That cleared up the mystery of why the new guy got the window seat.

But back to the catatonic boss...

It became important to me to learn what had triggered the Greek god's demise. What had set him off and turned him into stone with an iron grip? I wanted to figure out if it was something I might be able to avoid, or should I swap career paths and go into my backup profession—pin setter at the bowling alley?

As low man in the office, I got no facts...I got third-hand rumors. I don't like rumors, try not to listen to them, most often do not believe them. However, when all I had were rumors, the rumors became my facts.

The rumor (and I have no idea to this day if it was right or wrong) was that the one asshole in this office was the primary source of my hero's downfall. He had harassed and challenged and disrespected my hero so often that he just could not take it anymore and he had a nervous breakdown.

You know what...that rumor was enough for me...I did not like the guy anyway...he treated the women like shit and me like shit and fuck him. So, the lowest and least powerful person in the office...me...put together a plan to get rid of him...and it worked.

I had studied this guy carefully even before the startling event. He was an oddball. First off, he wore a hat. Who in California wears a hat...a real hat, like the kind Coach Bear Bryant wore at Alabama? Second, he brought his lunch to work in a paper bag...something I stopped doing in about second grade. Third, he suffered from migraine headaches. I assumed they were brought on by his idiotic behavior so I gave him no sympathy for their onset...and they were brutal.

My plan was multifaceted, and I put it in play immediately.

Step one...let's piss him off.

Every day he would come in, say something inappropriate to my women friends in our little work group, complain loudly about management and then get on the phone to start yelling at agents all day. How he was allowed to keep a job was beyond me...but no worries...I was going to step in and help management solve the problem.

He would open up his gray desk drawer and place his lunch in the bottom right drawer. In step one, I would wait for him to go to break, would open his drawer, crush his lunch and rush down to the break room to make sure I was seated next to him for our morning cup of coffee. This became important when he later found his crushed lunch and started trying to figure out who did this horrible crime. Not me, I was with him.

The lunch crushing went on for several days and then he had had enough of it. He started locking his desk. No problem, I think I figured out day one on the job that these cheap desks needed no key, you could open them just as easily with a letter opener...which I did...crushed his lunch...relocked the desk using the same letter opener...and ran down to join him for coffee.

He did everything he could to catch the crusher. He would pretend to go on break but hide around a corner and watch. He would ask a friend to watch for him...but I guess he never figured out he had no friends. I would go talk to them... we would make a deal that they would keep their mouths shut and I would crush away. Nothing worked for the guy and the crushing continued.

He finally could take no more and started hiding his lunch bag in the file cabinets...in the acres and acres of file cabinets that the office needed in those pre-digital days. The file area was supervised by my good friend T.D. who hired the most beautiful 18-year-old young women so he could later bed them, which he did. More on that later.

T.D. hated this guy as much as I did. So, with his help, I was invited to his daily team meetings where I would explain the situation to the ladies and offer $1 to whoever found the lunch and took me to it. This was a big hit. Fun for the ladies. Much more fun for me. Not so fun for the guy.

Every day he would hide his lunch in a new spot. Every day the ladies would find it and alert me. Every day I would come back and, to the great delight of the ladies, crush the asshole's lunch down into a wet flat mess.

Which takes me to stage two...

This asshole had an annoying habit. He would march into a manager's private office each morning and hang his hat on the hat rack, which was usually only used for raincoats and umbrellas in winter. Made no difference if the manager was holding a meeting or whatever, he marched in and hung his hat. The managers were being disrespected, but they were a very nice group and they put up with it... except one guy I grew to love who followed the asshole back out onto the floor and flung his hat at his desk like a Frisbee.

The hat was a very common hat. You could easily find an exact duplicate of it. I found two. One was WAY too big for him and one was WAY too small for him. However, they looked exactly alike on the hat rack.

The trigger for stage two action was the onset of a migraine. I would see him struggling. Recognized the actions he would take as he tried unsuccessfully to deal with it. And I could also tell when it was getting so bad that he would call his poor wife to come pick him up and take him home. He then made a trip into the men's room to cool down his face or whatever, and I sprang into action.

At the onset of the migraine, I would swap out his hat on the hat rack for the one that was WAY too small. When he put it on, it would perch up on his head like a thimble...the most ridiculous thing you have ever seen. I had bribed a secretary near that office to stop him and ask him if he was OK and to comment that it looked like his head was kind of swollen. That is how he went home...tiny hat stuck up on the top of his not really swollen head...migraine blaring away.

Next morning, he would be back at work as if nothing had happened. I am relentless, so I promise you that the lunch bag was in for a wonderful crushing that day. And sometime during that day, I would retrieve the tiny hat and replace it with the HUGE one...one that came down to his eyebrows when he put it on. I made sure that the same secretary commented to him as he walked out with the big hat that she could see the swelling had gone way down and she was glad he was feeling better.

Next morning, he got a crushed lunch and his regular hat back. And...repeat.

He quit within months. Everyone knew what I had been up to and I became a bit of a hero. The asshole was gone and the whole place felt better. But unfortunately, my buddy who supervised the file cabinet ladies was falling on difficult times.

His real name was not T.D. It was...well, let's call him Jerry. Jerry had banged every lady who ever worked there. He was tall and good-looking and young and he had the power to hire, promote and give raises. He used all his personal and business assets to supply himself with a very good sex life...in a manner that America has only recently begun to challenge.

Turns out not every young lady put up with his evil ways. One in particular—she had spent the night with him and next morning, she comes into the office half an hour late. He writes her up and lets her know that she will be fired next time she is late. She protests that the reason she was late was that he had kept her up all night. He explains carefully that that was then, and this is now...that was for fun and this is a business and not to test him in this area...he would fire her. She tested him. He fired her.

The women who worked in the file unit all met at a local hangout to wish her well and buy her a farewell drink (probably with the dollars they had made off of the lunch sack quest). She told them in great detail exactly what had happened. She also mentioned...over and over again...that he had the tiniest dick she had ever encountered. Now...many of the ladies knew whether or not that statement was true...I certainly don't...but they were all pissed off because basically the same thing had happened to all of them. And so, a name was born...T.D...for Tiny Dick.

The story and the name, T.D., spread through the office like wildfire. Within days, no one called him Jerry...everyone called him T.D. It finally got so bad, he quit. Karma...it can be a bitch.

I did not vanquish every asshole I ever met in the workplace. Some, in fact, vanquished me...or did me harm. Corporate life, especially if you are aiming for the top and are working in big corporations with lots of people and lots of egos...is a difficult arena. My hat...not the same hat that the asshole had in the story above... is off to those women and men who make it to the top. To get there, one has to find a way to deal with everyone, and very few find just the right formula.

CHAPTER THIRTY-THREE

Clearing the Air

I've written chapters in previous books about how to deal with a bad boss...again, something all of us get to experience at least once in a long career. I had not written previously about how to deal with troublesome co-workers. The example I have given you in the previous chapter would not be the example I hope you would use. I would hope you would work through the system, hold both the asshole and management accountable for their actions and BE UNAFRAID TO SPEAK UP. None of us deserve to be treated disrespectfully at work or anywhere.

Toward that end, I want to tell you how I handled these situations as a boss. There were many times when a group of employees would ask/demand to meet with me privately. Every one of those people...I love them forever...spoke up and let me know what was going on right under my nose. This became a call for action on my part to make my area of the company a better and more productive place to work...again, my thanks to those who complained.

Typically, I would say almost nothing. I would listen. I would, toward the end of the meeting, tell them clearly what I thought they had told me...so I knew, and they knew that I knew, what the problem was. I never promised to fix the problem in those meetings. What I always said is this..."Thank you. I understand completely. I do not believe in making promises. Actions are all that count. I have not had time to investigate this on my own or to determine the appropriate actions to take...I may have to bring experts in from legal or human resources to help me figure out the right thing to do. So, please do two things...accept my apology for letting this situation exist...and I mean that completely. I am embarrassed this is apparently going on during my watch. Second, let's get back together in two months...so you can tell me if the actions I have taken have been effective or not." They would always agree.

Nine times out of ten, they were complaining about an asshole who was doing what assholes do...sexually harassing, verbally abusing, taking advantage, failing to do their work, being disrespectful or maybe doing something that might be criminal...the last happened from time to time. I had a really good reputation for taking action. I earned that reputation. Always, when we met two months later, they would come into my office and tell me that we did not need to take time to have this meeting because the problem had long been resolved. I would thank them and that was that. Had they said nothing, that asshole would probably still be causing problems. I love the folks who stand up for themselves and others.

One time I did not follow the process I described above. The story will instantly reveal my lack of guts and my willingness to use my lofty position to make others do the difficult work.

I was new to a Midwest office. First few days on the job, a group of maybe a dozen ladies shows up at my office door and asks to come in. Standing room only...not that big an office. One of them closes the door...not a good sign. The spokesperson then proceeds to tell me about how they are all ready to boycott coming into the office and will do so if I do not take action. The guy who preceded me knew what was going on and did nothing despite their repeated requests. They want me to know they are dead serious this time and want something done pronto... they have had it.

Well, the preamble got my full attention. What was it? Turns out they worked with a woman who just plain smelled to high heaven all the time...and had for years. Stunk. Bad. They could take no more. I asked if they thought she had a medical problem. They said no, this was a hygiene problem...she wore the same clothes every single day...week after week...never washed, and they doubted she ever bathed.

By now I was sweating bullets. Telling a grown woman that she is going to have to do a better job with her personal hygiene was WAY out of my comfort zone.

I asked if she was any good at her job. They told me she was great at her job and they absolutely wanted her to stay in their unit, but they could not take another day of it. I gave them my standard "no promises" speech but did not say two months...I think I said two weeks. They left...probably unconvinced I would do anything. However, I think they were impressed when later that morning I made up some excuse and came over to ask the lady in question about some form. As I leaned in, I heard a little bit of chuckling behind me...and then it hit me...OH MY

GOD...this woman smelled to high heaven. I got what I needed from her and beat feet. They now knew I knew.

Not proud of this next move. I had one of the smartest, sharpest, nicest ladies working directly for me that you could ever dream of having on your team. And she had a high title, division manager. I asked my executive assistant to go get her. Within a minute, she was in my office. I explained the situation in full detail to her. I pretty much expected her to say..."Why are you pushing this stinker off on me... sounds like a job for the guy making the big bucks." But she did not. Instead, she said, "I got it." And off she went.

Toni handled that problem right then and there. She made up an excuse as to why the lady needed to come see her in her office. Praised her for her good work and told her that her co-workers often bragged on her. But before she let her go she said..."Well, this is kind of embarrassing, but you really don't smell fresh... anything going on...woman to woman?" The lady was completely surprised by this. She said she took a bath every week. Toni said that wasn't really enough given the high-pressured jobs we all had...she suggested bathing once a day. Toni then said that her clothes did not look too fresh. The lady admitted she never washed them...too busy. Toni assured her that having fresh clothes for each day was really mandatory at our company and could she please promise to change that habit? She assured Toni she would.

Guess what...the lady left there hugging Toni (I would have had to have a nose clip) and feeling great at all the praise she had gotten. She went back to her unit and thanked them for speaking so kindly about her...and told them that Toni was a hygiene nut and had convinced her to start taking more baths and cleaning her clothes and that she was going to take her up on her suggestions immediately.

When all of that got back to me...I about fell over. Toni was my new hero. She had handled a problem that seemed nearly impossible to me...handled it quickly, in a straightforward manner, directly and with a large amount of humanity thrown in. The other ladies in the unit spread the word that I was a man of action, that Toni was a saint, and we all lived happily ever after. Like I said...you can get a lot done when someone has the guts to put the truth on the table.

CHAPTER THIRTY-FOUR

Panty Drop at Work

I had my own moment at work when I had to deal with the impossible...

I was a brand new supervisor, age 21, in charge of a unit of about a dozen ladies. These were all veteran workers, dedicated, hard-working, smart ladies who, once again, had to suffer the indignity of working for a young, just barely out of college, man. Times were different then and they put away the feelings I am pretty sure they harbored and worked hard to make our unit, themselves, and me successful. It was my first "management" assignment and I am forever grateful for the grace they afforded me to learn, improve and eventually move up the ladder.

The job was a busy one, customer service and dealing with our wonderful, but often aggressive, insurance agents. The work was almost all done by phone and the phones never stopped ringing. The ladies went about their assignments very calmly and got the job done...day in and day out.

These ladies were normal. By that I mean they were people you might meet on the street or as neighbors or at school...people you would want to be friends with and be around. Each one was smart and they all knew how to do their jobs. I was the only newbie and they saw to it that I learned the ropes, and they did so in a manner that was, in retrospect, unbelievably respectful and kind...with a couple of exceptions I will mention.

At some point I decided that I could actually contribute to their work effort and maybe add some value. My first mission—help the one lady who was not very organized to become better organized. Well, that turned out to be a disaster. The other ladies watched without comment, smiles on their faces, quiet conversations taking place at breaks or after work. They knew this was not going to work...and it did not. Why did it not work? It had nothing to do with organizational skills and everything to do with the drinking problem that one lady had...a problem I was too young and inexperienced to recognize. Until...

Until one day, we were all working in our normal way when the unorganized lady jumped up from her desk and started shouting at the top of her lungs. Our office was one massive floor with maybe 500 identical desks on it and a bank of glass-walled offices for the executives over on one side. The shouting got everyone's attention...worker bees and execs.

Along with the shouting, the lady was jumping up and down and spinning around. This was quite a show...with me standing to the side not knowing what to do...hell, Einstein would not have known what to do. This little scene had to play itself out and then I would step in to see if I could help in the recovery. More screaming...more spinning. And then...and then she pulled up her skirt, threw off her shoes, pulled down her pantyhose and stepped completely out of them... leaving them in a heap as she took off running toward the bathroom.

There was dead silence. I asked two of the other ladies to follow her to see if they could be of some help and to then report back to me. Off they went. The only other thing I could think to do...with 500 sets of eyes silently watching me...was to go over to take a look at the pantyhose to see if they contained a clue as to her distress. They did.

In the absolute middle of the crotch of the panty part of the hose was...a giant earwig. It was alive and very active. An earwig is an insect about the size of two thumbnails that has a huge pincer, which apparently it had put to good use....thus the screaming, spinning and abandonment of the underwear.

I did not see my distressed worker again that day. She left for home immediately. I was left to sweep up the pantyhose, carefully remove the earwig, wash my hands several dozen times and try to return to my duty station looking like I had things under control. I believe that this was the happiest moment of the collective lives off all my other employees...as they got to see the new guy deal with the impossible. Fortunately, they never reminded me of this fiasco...at least not more than once or twice a day for as long as I knew them. "Hey, Mr. Hurzeler...find any earwigs today?"

I discovered later that the lady with the earwig panties had been drunk the night before. I am guessing she had stepped out of her pantyhose in what, given her messy desk at work, was probably her equally messy room at home...and that the earwig found a nice soft place to sleep. Then she must have hurriedly pulled on the same pantyhose the next morning before rushing off to work to try to conduct business with a bad hangover. That did not turn out so well for her or the earwig.

I provided at least two more moments of great hilarity for those ladies. One involved the first suit that I ever owned. I had shown up at work my very first day in a sport coat and slacks. HR (called Personnel in those days) sent me home immediately and told me not to return without a suit. So, off I went to J.C. Penney to buy two cheap suits...the only two suits anyone would see me in for about the next six months...we were beyond broke and I was making just enough to feed us, house us and get me back and forth to work.

About six months after I was hired, I went from my job as a clerk working alongside the ladies to being their supervisor. I had just graduated from college and the promotion came with the degree. I also got a $150-a-month raise...I was rolling in money now. I immediately bought a decent suit. Pretty proud of that suit. Maybe two weeks later, I was rushing (I am always rushing) around from one desk to another and a plastic name tag that was glued to the front of one of the desks...a hard piece of rectangular plastic with the name of the employee embossed on it...grabs my pants and rips them, leaving a gaping tear about nine inches long on the pant leg at my crotch. It makes a horrible sound and all the ladies stand up to see what had happened. The most senior and liveliest of the ladies, Elaine, looks at the tear and announces loudly, "Oh, my God, look how big it is." Since she was basically looking directly at my leg and underwear, everyone in the unit caught the humor in that statement and went into sustained convulsions of laughter. Me...not so much. I was off to find some duct tape for an emergency repair. Elaine always called me "Big Boy" after that...and I tried to get others to adopt it as my nickname, but they did not have the decency to go along with it.

And last, but not least. We had a really young and beautiful lady who was the area file clerk. She would go from desk to desk, gather up files and deliver them to wherever they were routed in the office...a beginner job for someone just out of high school. She wore the shortest skirts I have ever seen in an office. She was very well built and wore the loosest tops I have ever seen in an office. This lady was quite popular with all the guys. Heck, she was so much fun and so "innocent" that she was also popular with the ladies. And the ladies worked together to have her torture us.

The main scam was for the lady in front of me to put her files to be routed, not on her desk, but on the ground to the right of her chair. Here comes the young lady with the short skirt. She would bend over from the waist, which pulled her dress up to just about the top of whatever skimpy panties she would have on and her ass would be about two feet from my face. This all happened fast, so as she was bending over I would look up to see what I could see. I would see it in great detail...and then glance around to see a dozen ladies all looking directly at me with scorn etched heavily on their collective faces. I would turn red and go back to work. Later, I would hear the chuckling.

The alternate prank also had to be completely pre-arranged by the young lady and the ladies of my unit. It involved the young lady wearing a loose top dropping a file right next to me, bending over to get it so that her boobs basically hung there in space right before my eyes. Then I would glance up at the ladies who worked for me and they were all looking directly at me with...you guessed it...scorn etched heavily on their collective faces.

You know what? It has now been 50 years since I had my first management job...since I learned to supervise those older and wiser than I in as fair a way as I could think of at the time...in a unfair environment where men were treated very differently from women...in a pressure cooker where I was so inexperienced that I had to read manuals and humbly ask for help to get problems resolved...where I was allowed to make rookie mistakes and painfully learn from them without building up animosities that lasted a lifetime...where I came to learn the importance of EVERY worker in an organization, from top to bottom. And speaking of bottoms... whoops, lost track there for a moment.

So I am grateful to this day for the ladies of the Commercial Service Unit...for their humor and hard work and for putting me on a path that led me to whatever business success I have enjoyed.

CHAPTER THIRTY-FIVE

My Secretary...Centerfold for *Playboy* Magazine

I had an executive assistant for each job I had from about age 30 up until my retirement at a little over 60 years of age. Without exception, they were outstanding human beings and helped me to get my job done much more efficiently and better than I could have managed on my own. I am guessing that with today's cell phones, email, texting, conferencing, electronic calendars and speech-to-writing technology, executive assistants may not be needed as much at some levels as they once were...but I could not have done without them during my career. I love them all.

I had one executive assistant back in 1980 who was much older than I. She was a dream assistant. I would come back from trips and she would bring in a stack of thank-you letters to people I had visited on my trip...all typewritten and ready for my signature...WOW! She figured out things before I even knew I needed them... and took action. I thought the world of her...still do.

The company I worked for owned a major piece of an airline...a start-up airline. It had a small first class section and we always got to fly first class...often as the only travelers in that part of the plane. This was back in the days when you would be asked, "Would you like the steak or the lobster...or both?" And the booze flowed.

Well, the booze apparently flowed a bit too much for me on one trip. A couple of weeks later, my long-time executive assistant comes in and hands me a business card...the card of a flight attendant for the airline we partly owned. My assistant said, "The beautiful young lady in the lobby said that you told her to look you up next time she had a layover in Chicago and today is the day. Do you want me to call Linda and have her set another spot at the dinner table?"

Whoops. Yeah...yet another reason to quit drinking...God knows what all I have told people while drunk. I was horrified...as well I should have been. My assistant just stared at me. I asked her if she could explain to the young lady that she...my assistant...worked for a fool who had apparently had too much to drink and that I was married with kids and then repeat the part about my being a fool and see if she could get her to go away. My assistant did not say a word...but took off to talk to the flight attendant and never ever mentioned it to me again. Didn't need to...I had learned my lesson. And...I think I managed never to fly that airline again. Shameful...but that is what drinking could do to me. I gave it up about that time.

Not all my assistants were older than I. I had a couple who were much younger. One provided me with the surprise of my life. She came into my office one day, closed the door and popped open the current issue of *Playboy*. The centerfold unfolded and...it was her...absolutely naked. I about had a heart attack...for several reasons...but mostly because it was so inappropriate and was going to cause me a major problem at work...oh, and she was beautiful all dressed up in her smile.

I actually stammered...not being able to form a sentence. She jumped in and said, "Don't worry, it is not me...it is my identical twin sister." That did not calm me down.

The very next weekend, we were all at a pool party thrown by someone at work. She got out of the pool, after having consumed maybe one too many margaritas, and playfully sat herself down in her wet bikini in my lap right next to where my wife was sitting. That did not play well at home.

So, in one of the more brilliant moves of my life, the next Monday I arranged for her to get a promotion to work for a guy who was very interested in her. She was happy. The guy was happy. Linda was happy. I was happy. So...win/win.

I still have a copy of that issue of *Playboy*, as it had some wonderful cartoons and stories in it that I like to revisit from time to time.

One other story along these lines. I worked alongside a guy who I felt was one of the most average-looking guys I had ever met. This was in Southern California and this guy was from a southern state originally and did not look like a Southern California guy at all...he looked out of place. He was one of the most interesting guys I had ever met. For one thing, he had been married 10 times and had divorced each wife when she reached 21 years of age or so...he being in his late 40s or maybe 50 when I first met him. In fact, before I knew his history, my wife and I had arranged to go on an early morning fishing trip with him. When he arrived, I greeted him and asked him his daughter's name. Yup...not his daughter...his wife. Ouch!

He and I would travel together. I knew the territory and he did not, so I would pick the hotels we where we would stay and the places we would dine. First night on the road, he and I are having dinner. He tended to sweat when he drank and was sitting there eating way too much...which I think contributed to him being overweight...and he was kind of shiny from the booze sweat...a mess if you ask me. This lady comes over to our table and hands me a note. I open it and it reads, "Hey, good looking, finish that meal and come join me in my room...Room #723. XXXOOO Jenna."

I look up at the lady somewhat flustered...this had never before happened to me in my entire life. As I caught her eye, she motioned to me to pass the note along...it was for my friend...not me. He read it, wiped the food off his mouth and the sweat off his brow and announced, "Don, could you get the bill; I have to leave now." And off they went.

Every time we traveled, something similar happened. Heck, I was married, so that was fine with me. But guess what, he was married too...to the child bride back home...the soon-to-be ex-#10.

This went on for months. My ego was dust. He continued to look unhealthy, unfit, and unattractive and turned out to be the greatest chick magnet I have ever been around. I will never understand it.

Then one day my secretary comes into my office and closes the door. She was fresh out of high school, maybe 18, beautiful, a devote churchgoer, shy, never mentioned a boyfriend, friendly but all business. I would have bet money that she was a virgin...but that was never any of my concern or my business. So...what news could this youngster have for me? You guessed it. She wanted to let me know that she was dating the chick magnet...whose office was three down from mine.

Silence from me as my electrical circuits tried to deal with this revelation. I mentioned that he was probably 30 years older than she. She said she recognized that and liked mature men (well, she might have a surprise coming about how "mature" he was). I then mentioned that he was married. She knew that too and said he was going to divorce his wife soon and marry her. I mentioned that he had been married something like ten times and her marriage to him would be his eleventh. She replied that she knew that and that it would be "his eleventh and last."

The chick magnet divorced wife number ten and I believe she continued her pursuit of her GED. He married my secretary. Guess what...last time I checked, they were still very happily married. All I can say is that it took him forever, but he finally got it right. My secretary was and is a winner and I am glad he settled down with her.

CHAPTER THIRTY-SIX

Fun on Stage

I love being on stage speaking to an audience or participating in a conversation with others on a panel or round table...love it. I am a ham. The audience is pretty much captive. Fun times, indeed.

I know a lot of people hate being up in front of a few people or a few thousand people. Not me. I will tell you why. I made an agreement with myself long ago that whatever happens onstage is OK. If a joke flops or I forget a line or a name or lose my place in the script...life goes on. It is what it is. I grade each presentation from A-plus to F and make some mental notes of what worked and what did not...and go on to the next one.

An aside on why speaking publicly was and is so easy and comfortable for me.

First, I almost never use any notes of any kind. If I do use notes, they are often on one small card and may just be three or four words written in large letters so I can glance down to remember what comes next. Most of the time...no notes at all. This works for me whether the speech is just five minutes or more than an hour. No notes.

Second, no props. The biggest prop ever invented by mankind is the PowerPoint presentation. I know the whole world uses it...part of the culture. I never use it because it takes the attention away from the speaker (that would be me...the big ham), it is often boring as hell, it is too detailed, and the biggest problem of all...it is subject to technical difficulties. I cannot tell you how many presentations I have seen go down in flames as the speaker tries to get his or her laptop to connect with the projector or can't find the file, or you name it. I hate PowerPoint. Post something online and give people the link if you want them to have information after the presentation...but spare me the reading of the damn PowerPoint...speaker facing the screen and not the audience...reading the damn thing word for word...accidentally hitting the back key rather than the forward key. The best part of being retired is I will never have to watch another PowerPoint presentation.

Reminds me of a presentation I was asked to give in northern California. There would be three of us speaking over the course of the afternoon. The organizer asked if any of us would be using PowerPoint. The guy from a rival company said he would...64 screens worth of information. The organizer then asked me when I would like to go on (I was the president of the organization and got first choice). I said, "Right after him." What a great choice...his presentation was a disaster. I started off by saying, "You can bring up the lights, I don't have a PowerPoint," and got a big round of applause. Oh, how I hate PowerPoint.

Third, I prepare. I almost always try to get to the exact place I will be speaking, get into position long before anyone arrives and give my presentation several times to an empty room or to the people setting up for the event. I am ready.

Fourth, I speak as if I am in a conversation with a single person. I move out to as close to the audience as I can get...love the kind of microphones that clip on and are wireless...hate the ones that are on a stick and not going anywhere. I like to roam around and stay in eye and physical contact with the audience.

And fifth...oh, I mentioned this one already...it is what it is. My day will continue on just fine if I screw something up. And as I said, 99% of the time I do not screw anything up and the whole thing is just a big-time pleasure.

As an executive, as a volunteer in numerous charitable organizations, as a mentor and teacher, and as a leader in a 20,000-plus professional organization with chapters all over the U.S. and overseas...I got a chance to speak at least 1000 times during my 40-year career.

Over the years, 99% of my speeches or other stage appearances have been really good...some excellent. But there have been others...

A classic flop for me took place in Milwaukee. I was up in front of 800 people and was leading a professional pledge that involved virtually everyone in the audience joining in and following along. I had everyone stand up, place their right hand in the air and repeat after me...

Now, this pledge is something I had either taken or led hundreds of times. That particular year I gave that pledge maybe three times a week. It is not overly long. I had been participating in the pledge for about 30 years. I knew the pledge.

However, on this day I tripped myself up. I got everyone up with their right hands in the air and asked them to repeat after me. I launched into the pledge, pausing for them to repeat what I had just said. When I got to the part that says, "I shall strive to ascertain and understand the needs of others...," I thought to myself, "Man, this whole thing has gone well. What a beautiful room here at the Pfister Hotel. What a great day. I wonder if I should end this part with the story about being mistaken for the limo driver." As that thought passed, I looked out at the silent audience and realized that I had completely forgotten my place in the pledge. They were silent. I was silent. We all had our right hand in the air. They knew I was screwed and...I was. So, without further hesitation I said, "And Amen." Trust me, "and Amen" is in no way part of the pledge. But it was that day.

I got a great explosion of laughter and it was all OK.

Later in the program, I was seated next to the podium and a stuffed-shirt CEO of the highest caliber was giving his keynote presentation. He read every damn word of it off of the typed script that his speech writer had prepared for him. Big time snore. Toward the end, he told a joke...poorly. He was so proud of himself that he had thought to throw in this joke, but the audience had long since been in stun mode and NO ONE got the joke. Not one person out of the 800 people there even snickered...silence. The speaker panicked and turned to me. I got up and grabbed the microphone and said, "Don't ask me why your joke bombed, I couldn't even remember the damn pledge." Second biggest laugh of the day. The speaker was not one of those enjoying the moment.

I mentioned that I hate PowerPoint. I also hate teleprompters. I recognize their usefulness, but I hate them. I believe that they make every single speaker the same...average. Look to the left. Look to the right. Look straight ahead. Robotic.

I managed to avoid them most of my life. However, sometimes they are unavoidable. So, I got a coach and got good at doing the teleprompter thing. Translation...I too could be average. Usually when I used the teleprompter, things went OK...but there was this one time...

I was president of a professional organization. We had our annual big deal meeting...thousands in attendance, including my entire family. This was my time to shine...and I did. For three or four days, I would be led from one venue or meeting room to the next and give talks lasting from five minutes to an hour. Most of the time I had no notes at all. But two of the longest ones were highly scripted and required a teleprompter. The first one went great. The second...not so much.

I was told to show up at a certain time and sit on stage with a dozen others under the hot lights. One by one they gave their talks. By the time I was on (and

I was the closer), I was hot, tired and dry. The teleprompter was arranged nicely and I launched into my part...a presentation written for me that I had never seen. I remember thinking...damn, this thing is LONG. At just about that moment, my mouth went entirely dry.

Unless you have been up in front of a large group, some of whom were industry CEOs that you would kind of like to impress, and you have had your mouth go entirely dry, you have no idea what a bad feeling that is. No problem, I had requested a bottle of water to be placed under the podium and I was very at ease saying, "Excuse me a second, I need a drink of water." So, I tried to keep talking, which was getting harder to do because my mouth was like a sand box at this point. I groped around for that water bottle with no luck. Finally, I stopped abruptly (this always drives the person operating the teleprompter crazy because he or she has to make sure it is in just the right spot when the speaker is ready to resume) and started reaching for the water...normally at first and then in full emergency mode because I could not find it. After many long and awkward moments...with my son looking up at me like, "Can I just hide under my chair now?" someone brought me a bottle of water and I was back in business.

I thanked the gentleman for the water. Apologized for the awkward delay and launched back into the speech. I said exactly seven more words...and a huge fireworks display went off all around me. I had reached the end of the speech and the fireworks were the big finish. I had not been warned about the fireworks and was surprised as hell that the speech was over. Seven more words and I could have beat feet out of there to the bar. Instead...time to remember the rule about "it is what it is." It has been fifteen years since that moment and I still need to remind myself of the rule. And despite my rule and my normal strict adherence to it... having just re-lived the debacle in writing this story, I will have a hard time getting to sleep tonight. Damn.

Like I said, most of the time things went well and the audience and I both made the best of it. But things happen on the way to events from time to time. Example...

I gave a talk in Chicago one evening. It was a lot of fun because not only were my wife and friends from work there, one of my oldest friends in the world just showed up from Colorado. Steve Goppert was in town, heard I was speaking and showed up...and I was delighted.

After the talk, Linda and I ran to the airport for an overnight flight to Los Angeles. I was to speak in L.A. the next day at noon. Since I was originally from Los Angeles and still had lots of friends there, I invited a whole table full to join us for the lunch...and my keynote, one-hour speech. I was really well prepared and could hardly wait for this chance to kind of show off and be the big star of the event.

Everyone showed up. Ten minutes before I was to go on, the head organizer for the event pulled me aside and said that they were horribly behind and needed to cut my keynote down from one hour to ten minutes. Ouch! Then...he said, "Oh, and can you use part of those ten minutes to read these names, have the person come up to the stage where you will hand them this certificate they earned and have their photo taken with you?" There were 22 names. Worse yet, these folks had been part of a sponsored program for immigrants from both Southeast Asia and India...and I was to read their names without any practice...and they were the most difficult names (for me) that I had ever read.

So...I was introduced ("And now, here is Don Hurzeler to hand out our certificates.") and the stage was mine. I said "Ladies and gentlemen, we will now begin the butchering of the names." And I launched into my pitiful attempt at getting the names right. We made it into a bit of a fun thing...I would mess them up...they would correct me...I would then ask them how to pronounce the next name...they would have no idea...and repeat. It was fun and respectful...may not sound that way, but it was and I got the job done. My ten minutes were up...and then some...and before I could launch into any abbreviated remarks, my host was at my side grabbing the microphone.

I was steaming mad. I told my guests I had to run to the airport. Truth is, I had to get out of there before I said something I would regret. I grabbed Linda and double timed it out to our rental car. Just as I was about to make a clean escape, the idiot who was my host that day...the guy who invited me to fly overnight cross country and pay for a table for my friends so they could hear me butcher 22 names... the one who cut my "keynote" to ten minutes and then threw in the certificate ceremony for free...came running out into the parking lot waving his arms and shouting. I had no choice but to stop and roll down the window...perhaps to hear a heartfelt apology. Nope...no apology. I had left so quickly that he had not been able to give me my speaker's gift...which he handed to me all nicely wrapped. I thanked him and told him I had to hurry to the airport.

Somewhere along the way to the airport, Linda opened the gift. It was...I promise...an 8x10" framed and autographed photo of the idiot host. It never made it onto the plane.

And then there was snow. I flew from Chicago to a big city in the Southwest (I don't want to embarrass anyone on this one...don't care if I embarrassed anyone on the previous one). It was horrible weather in Chicago...snow and ice. However, after hours of delays, we took off. We were the last plane to land in the Southwest city before snow and ice closed that airport...just barely made it.

I went out front where I was to meet my ride. No ride. This presented a bit of a problem because it was late and I did not know where they were taking me for the night. For reasons I cannot remember, I did not have the number of the person organizing the meeting the next day. Panic. I did remember a friend who was part of that organization and called him. He called the head guy and the head guy called me back. I asked him who was picking me up. They guy said..."I thought you knew, we canceled the meeting due to the snow storm. It looks like all air travel in and out will be shut down for two days...don't come." Well, I told him, I did not know because no one told me and I was now at their airport. Net result...I slept on the floor of the airport that night and did not get home for 36 hours...after giving no speech.

The other 99% of the time, I was treated like royalty. People went way out of their way to make me feel at home, take me to ball games, introduce me to new friends and their families, explore the local sights. These people gave me the opportunity to speak in all fifty states of our great country. They are my friends to this day (except the idiot in Los Angeles). And on top of it all...they let me be a ham on stage...and I loved it. No regrets (well, that one with the missing bottle of water and the big ending screwed up) and lots of good memories. I love being on stage.

CHAPTER THIRTY-SEVEN

Don Hurzeler, Stud Muffin

I fly. By that, I mean, I have spent a lifetime on airplanes. I would often travel well over 100,000 miles a year by plane, most of it domestically. One year I flew something like 250,000 miles, when I was the national head of a large insurance professionals' organization. I fly.

I have been to over 100 countries. Flown airlines you have never heard of to places I had never heard of. Since retiring a dozen years ago, the places we go are more and more exotic. Lots of time in an airplane.

I am not spoiled about anything in life except my wife, my cameras, my surfboards and air travel. I like first class...sorry if that sounds elitist...it is. But I spent so many years crammed into the middle seat in economy between a drunk guy and a kid that I feel I have earned the good seat...thus the terms "entitled" or "privileged." You will hate me for this...my best friends know I have a term for those in economy..."The Others." Yup...spoiled rotten, mostly by United Airlines, whom I love.

I once saw a young couple think they were fooling people and sneak one by one into the bathroom on the way to Hawaii to become members of the Mile-High Club...no, wait a minute...that was us.

Over the decades, I have seen it all. And in the course of all this, I got to know each plane and how to make the best of each plane configuration. Case in point...

I had had a long day in Tampa Bay. I was there, after traveling down from Chicago, for a spring training baseball game. The game got rained out. I then headed to the airport and took one wrong turn and was on a miles-long bridge across the bay...no way to turn around. I had to drive all the way across, turn around and drive all the way back, missing my flight by just minutes...oh, this day was not going well. The next flight to Chicago was in six hours (bunch of flights canceled due to weather in Chicago). I had turned in my car and so I was just plain stuck...for six damn hours. By the time the plane took off, it was already late in Chicago and I was exhausted...a full day of travel and frustration and no joy.

The captain came on as soon as we took off. Weather in Chicago. Our hour and half flight might be three hours...or we might have to land in Milwaukee and bus back to O'Hare. This was turning into a classic bad travel day.

I decided to sleep. I left my nice seat and worked my way to the back of the plane. This was, I think, an L1011 or DC10 craft that had a middle section in economy with four or five seats and arm rests that you could move up out of the way. I grabbed a magazine to cover my eyes and lay down for a nice nap before arriving home or wherever.

I slept like a baby. It was warm. The only good I ever got out of *Time* magazine was that it kept the light out of my eyes that night, with the magazine spread open to some colorful photo of the Kentucky Derby or some other typical subject. I stayed asleep until we were ready to land. The flight attendant gently woke me up in the lights-out back of the plane and I returned to my seat, where she promptly filled my request for a cup of hot coffee.

I got back in my regular seat and got ready to land; we were halfway down to the ground already. Pretty soon, I felt the engines rev up and we began to gain altitude. The pilot came on to inform us that we had been waved off due to icy conditions at O'Hare and that we were going to circle one more time in hopes of getting an OK to land. If we did not get it, we would have to divert to Milwaukee immediately because we were quite low on fuel.

At this, the guy in front of me went into a fit. He started jamming himself into the back of the seat and making that seat fly into me. I still had my tray down and a cup of coffee on that tray and after about the third time he slammed into the back of his seat, I was wearing the hot coffee.

I grabbed the back of his seat and shook it like a paint-mixing machine. I was one pissed off dude. Well, so was he...and he popped up like a jack-in-the-box to confront me. He took one look at me and a look of terror came across his face and he just plain melted back into his seat. I could not even see the top of his head...and the seat stayed dead still. This guy had taken one look at my macho self and knew that I was not to be messed with. Got to admit...it kind of pumped me up.

We did land after that one last circle and all was well. I had hoped to pop up first when the seat belt light went off so I could get out in the aisle and glare once again at the nincompoop. As I started to get up, I could tell others felt my strength and perhaps saw my anger and they too turned away from me, wanted nothing to do with me. Stud...I was an absolute stud and they could all sense that fact...loved it. The guy cowered in his seat, would not even look up at me.

I exited the plane under full steam. The crowd literally parted as I made my way to my limo. People wanted out of my way. When I got to the limo, the driver could also sense my power and he too fell silent for the whole drive home. This day was ending much better than it had started.

Once home I tried to sneak into bed, but Linda heard me and asked if it was me. I was still pumped up and said something stupid like..."You were expecting someone else at this hour?"

I asked if I could turn on the light...she said yes...and I did.

Linda said, "Oh Don, you've been in a fight!" I smiled and said no, her stud-muffin had not been in a real fight but had stood up for all that was right and vanquished the rude and weak. She then asked how come my face was so badly bruised. I told her it must be the light, I was fine. She said I was in no way fine, to go look in the mirror.

Turns out that *Time* magazine on my sweaty face for more than an hour in the back of the plane had transferred the red and purple ink from that photo spread onto my entire face. My face looked like a throbbing hematoma. I looked like a monster out of a movie. No wonder everyone avoided me...I looked like I was dying of bubonic plague.

The end of my days as a stud-muffin.

CHAPTER THIRTY-EIGHT

A Giant Wave of Emotion

When you get old, things happen to you that you never expected. I never expected to have so much of my life in the past...and so much past to look back on. I am a guy who lives in the present and the future...I feel it is really important to always have something to look forward to. So, I do not spend much time in the past. But... every now and again...

I just watched a thing that Paul McCartney and James Corden did for James's TV show and it was a segment of Carpool Karaoke. I have a tiny connection to that because my cousin, David Kahne, was part of the team that helped put together that segment. David has produced Paul and often works as the sound man on Paul's amazing projects all over the world. To say I am proud of my cousin would be one of the world's biggest understatements...I am in awe of his talents. If you ever get the chance, look up the Carpool Karaoke segment on YouTube and watch it...fantastic.

Now, why would that make me emotional? Because watching it brought back a flood of great memories.

Dan Fairbanks was one of my best friends. I kept my surfboard under his house, close to the beach in Palos Verdes. We went to church together, played sports together, surfed together, were in the same classes...you name it. When it came time to go to college, we got an apartment together and moved out to the San Fernando Valley. Later he was in my wedding, and he was there the days my son and daughter were born. I was with him as his parents died and shortly before he died. Danny was my brother and I will always miss him.

His family had been so kind to me growing up. They were wealthy by my family's standards and had a place out near Palm Springs. I would get invites to go out and play golf at a private course and see how the rich people lived. Later in life I wanted to repay some of that kindness, and I did. I arranged to meet my three best friends—Danny, Tom and Mike—in Atlanta to celebrate our all turning 60, and for us all to be there on the day the first of us, Danny, turned 60. What I did not tell them ahead of time was that we would not just be playing golf and going out to dinner, I had gotten us tickets to the Masters Tournament in Augusta and we were going to attend. It was fantastic.

We had lots of adventures with Danny boy. I took him on a fishing expedition in the way back of Wyoming. He, Linda and I chased sharks and dolphins in Hawaii...lots of fun.

So, one time, when he was living almost on the sand in Hermosa Beach, California, and we were living in the northwest suburbs of Chicago, I got this great idea. I called him up, told him I was sending him a very specific airline ticket...don't mess with it...get on that plane. Told him to bring his clubs for a long weekend of golf at my club. Told him that I was traveling on the day he arrived and that I would meet him in baggage at O'Hare Airport and that Linda would then pick us up and take us downtown for a concert...gave him no further details. He was in.

It all went according to plan. We got in the car and drove to the United Center where the Chicago Bulls play...seats something like 23,000 for concerts. There were no signs outside indicating who was playing, nor had we told Danny. Soon enough, we came across a stylized sign that he immediately recognized as Paul McCartney playing a guitar. He turned to me looking stunned..."Is Paul McCartney going to be here?" I said I thought he was going to be here. Dan then said, "This arena is huge, will we be able to see him?" I showed him the tickets...row V V...that did not look too promising.

We made our way down the arena floor. We found row V...way up in the back, but we could not find row V V. After quite a bit of looking, and following my male mindset of never asking for directions or help, I suggested we just do this systematically...start in the front row and work our way back till we found it. It was agreed and off we went.

Turns out V V was the front row. Turns out our seats were in the middle of that front row. Why? Because my cousin and his wife had set it all up for us.

When Paul came out on stage, he bent over in front of us and said, "Good evening." I thought Danny boy would pass out. Greatest night out of his or our lives. Thank you, Paul. Thank you, David and Ava.

I wasn't responsible for all the surprises in our relationship. In fact, Danny often surprised me...sometimes good...sometimes not so good...one time great... one time tragic.

The good...he always had presents for Linda and good stuff for me...they were just constants. If I wrote a book, he bought dozens of copies and gave them out to his friends. He always wanted me to succeed and went out of his way to make that happen.

The bad...he loved my folks and came up to see them one day when my dad was starting to fail...Dad being over 90 at the time. I heard Danny say, "So, Jim, do you still have all those guns?" Oh my God, you could not have asked a more dangerous question. Dad got up and disappeared to the back room as I tore into Danny. I reminded Dan that my dad was old and shaky and not to be fully trusted anymore...especially with a gun. I also reminded him that he did not have a gun... he had an arsenal. I then reminded him that Dad always kept each gun loaded, one in the chamber, and that he had long ago filed off any safety latches. Dan was about to have a wonderful session with a shaky old man with maybe two dozen different guns...from 22s to shotguns. I wished him good luck and went out to the garage. I waited for the gunshot, but thankfully it never came.

The tragic...I was with him when he got a death sentence from a doctor...a particularly nasty type of cancer. Gave him no time at all. We cried through lunch and then he asked me to circle the date on my calendar, but one year from now. He promised to be alive and able to travel to Hawaii in one year...maybe nine months more than they had given him...and promised me he would be there. True to his word...he made it...and maybe a year or two more. Fought like a son of a gun and then called me to let me know the fight was over. Broke my damn heart and brings tears as I write this.

So, I saved the best for last. Danny had a girlfriend in junior college, Pam Mashburn. She was perfect. I loved her. He loved her more. She was beautiful, smart, happy, fit and loved a good laugh, which Dan and I provided in spades.... What more could a guy ask for than a girl who thinks your stupid jokes are funny? Danny and she were an item just about every day for something like two years.

After our two junior college years, Dan headed off to USC and I headed off to Chapman University. There were no text messages or email back then... and good luck trying to call someone in college...none of us were ever in our dorm rooms. So, I doubt that I spoke to Danny until maybe Christmas. "How is Pam?" I asked. "Don't know," says Dan, "we broke up." I was astonished...and never got a good explanation as to why. He never mentioned her again. Pam disappeared from my life too, leaving a void and a whole bunch of unanswered questions.

Not too long ago, Dan came over to Hawaii to spend Christmas with Linda and me. He was by himself. He had never married. Dated a long list of beautiful and bright women...and had a special one from his days in Tahiti...but she had gotten married to someone else and he just never did. One night at dinner he tells Linda and me that he has one regret in his life...that he never married. Kind of a downer moment that quickly passed and we were on to some other topic.

Flip forward maybe six months. I am at my folks' house in Palos Verdes, which is not far from where Danny lived in Hermosa Beach. He knows I am in town, calls up and asks if he can come up right now. He drives up and there is someone in the car...and I recognize her immediately...it is Pam Mashburn. I about fell down the front stairs.

Pam, who now had a different last name from a previous marriage, looked SENSATIONAL. I think she weighed less than she did in college, was fit and beautiful...quite an achievement since she was now 60-something. Everything about her looked good and young and happy.

Dan was beaming. Turns out that he had been out in Indian Wells to buy a second house and worked with a real estate agent who had lived in the area for a long time. Coincidentally, she had graduated from Palm Springs High School, as did Pam. The light went off in Dan's head, so he asked if she knew Pam Mashburn, and she did. Dan blurted out...is she married? She was not...divorced and single. Dan asked for her phone number and got it. He called her for the first time in 45 years...45!

Pam answered the phone and he said, "Hello, Pam, this is Dan Fairbanks." Dan said there was quite a long pause and then she said, "I'm listening." Well, you know where this story is going.

They had been dating for about three months when Dan calls me up and invites me to breakfast, saying that he has an announcement that the two of them want to share with me first. So when we met, Dan asked me if I could venture a guess. I said, "Let me guess, Dan...you're pregnant?" Not a bad guess considering the beer belly he had put on over the years. "Nope!" he replied. "Not me, but we'll work on that after we get married." Pam laughed at our banter and stupid jokes that had not changed in 45 years.

The wedding invitation had the cutest photos on it you have ever seen...I think they were the only two photos they had of themselves from about 1966, taken in a photo booth...used to be you could get four tiny photos for a quarter or whatever.

Opposite were photos of them in the same poses today...Pam looking exactly as she did in the '60s and Dan taking up quite a bit more space than he did 45 years prior, but still a good-looking stud. Of course Linda and I attended their wedding at Palos Verdes Country Club, along with numerous friends who had to see the woman who finally inspired Dan to say, "I do." He was the happiest I have ever known him to be.

They had a dream life, but then six months after their wedding the damn cancer made its presence known and it all came to a halt. But nothing could stop the love. He was given six to twelve months to live but survived another two-and-a-half years. They didn't want it to end. Like I said...broke my heart.

Dan was so lucky to be supported by Pam in those difficult days. She did a great job. He knew it. We knew it. Pam is our hero and best friend for life. Sad end to a great love story that deserves to be told...a happy ending followed by a damn poor surprise. I am forever happy that he found her again. And so was he. Life can be so bittersweet.

So, that is the problem with getting old...either you die, or your friends or relatives die. But, as Tupac so wisely points out, life goes on. I have learned to keep my eyes focused on now and what lies ahead...and every now and again, to remember the past...guts, feathers and all. I am thankful for every moment of my life...even the toughest parts. Life is good.

CHAPTER THIRTY-NINE

My 14-Year Run Attending the NFL Pro Bowl in Honolulu

Have you ever met anyone so selfish that they would leave their family behind in Illinois in mid-winter and attend the NFL Pro Bowl in Honolulu by themselves, 14 years in a row? Well, now you have.

I wrote a whole chapter in a previous book trying to justify this selfishness (no one was convinced), so I will not repeat it here. However, I will tell you how much fun it was and hope that my wife, son and daughter decide to not read this book.

I did not go to Oahu each year to go to the Pro Bowl—that was a side benefit. I went to Hawaii each winter to go surfing. The surf is great in Hawaii in February. The weather is perfect. I needed a break from everything...and I took it. I did not travel with my buddies or bring my golf clubs or go on tours...I surfed all day every day, partied all night every night with the NFL All-Stars and media people...and repeat.

There was a surf contest at that time of year that was the most laid-back contest ever and it was at Makaha. One does not just waltz into Makaha and go surfing looking as pale as I looked...unless they know you. They knew me. They did not necessarily know me by name, but they knew I showed up every year with a trunk full of beer and that I knew how to surf well enough to stay the heck out of everyone's way. I kind of got a pass to be there and over the years, I like to think they eventually enjoyed my annual visit. I know I did.

So, I surfed Makaha if the waves were not too big. I also surfed Haleiwa, if those waves were not too big. On very rare occasions I tried other spots, but that never seemed to go very well. The worst of those mistakes was my paddling out at a place I knew was very "local" back then. I knew about local...I grew up in Palos

Verdes and there is a movie about the surf community there...a piece of shit movie called the Tribes of Palos Verdes. I was not one of the Bay Boys. But I did know what "local" looked like and could be a bit territorial myself if someone came in and was rude or unskilled...putting us all in danger in the surf.

So, at age 55, without a bit of color on my skin, as I was living full time in Chicago and had not surfed for a year, I get the bright idea to paddle out, all by myself, at Velzyland. I can hear my surfing buddies laughing out loud right now. This was a plain stupid idea.

I parked my all-white "stand out like a sore thumb" perfectly clean rental sedan near Velzyland (which is on the northwest side of the North Shore area of Oahu), waxed up my board (at least I had my own board and it was not a tanker like they would rent you in those days) and paddled out...surf looked great.

I noticed a dozen guys in the lineup, and they were ripping it. I also noticed that one of them was done and headed in. He was about 21 years old and looked like he lived on that surfboard. He did not say a word but paddled quickly in my direction. When he got to me, he threw his legs down into the water on each side of his board, sat up and punched me as hard as he could directly in my nose. No words said...one punch...gone.

The punch broke my nose. Did I mention I was 55 at the time? Asshole. I had expected the normal..."Hey, haole boy, you need to be surfing back at Waikiki... you not welcome here." I did not expect to get sucker-punched directly in the nose.

He headed for the beach. Took me a minute to recover and I had a decision to make...I could go after him (I wanted nothing to do with that guy...he would pound me into poi) or I could continue on and get a wave or two so I could say I had surfed Velzyland. I chose to surf.

The guys in the lineup were nearly bent over laughing at me. I think they were startled to see how badly I was bleeding and maybe how old I was. Whatever, they turned their backs and reduced their laughter to a mild chuckle. No one said a word.

I am sure they felt sorry for me, so they let me catch a wave. I caught a decent wave and did a decent job on it. When I finally kicked out at the end of the wave, I was closer to the beach than the lineup and starting to think about sharks and all the blood, so I decided to call it a bad day.

When I got to the beach, I looked for the guy...and thankfully he was gone. I went to my rental car and found it where I left it, but with every single piece of glass broken out of the car...windows, lights, mirrors...and, quite notably, the windshield...completely gone. Welcome to paradise.

Ever try to drive to the hospital in a car with no windshield and a horrible bloody nose? That car looked like slaughterhouse when I finally returned it to the rental place...and paid whatever deductible I had to pay. Not my best Pro Bowl experience.

And not my only odd experience. I was at Planet Hollywood one night in Waikiki. I was at the bar having a beer. A very nice-looking young lady sat down next to me and started to chat me up. I have to admit, I thought she was a hooker, so I only mildly engaged her in conversation. It was a bit late and the TV was on behind the bar...and my hero, Johnny Carson, was doing his show. The Beach Boys came out and played "Kokomo." The lady seemed very pleased...turned out she wrote "Kokomo." I'm impressed, tell me more. Well, this gal knew everyone in Hollywood...simply amazing. I asked if she knew Johnny Carson...she did...they were best of friends...would I like to meet him? Well, of course I would like to meet him...when and how? She said we would have to wait until next break, and she would introduce me. This confused me a bit...how would she manage that...by phone? Oh no, we can talk right through the TV...she talks to him almost every night directly through the TV. I had the full attention of a woman who was just plain bat shit crazy. I think I used the old "I have to hit the head" excuse to get the heck out of there.

One more mention of a story I had in my last book, so I will keep it quick. It was on one of these Pro Bowl trips when I paddled out at Haleiwa in a roaring rain and windstorm and got surrounded by a huge number of silky sharks that were actually feeding on the debris line from the river that runs into the bay there. There were enough sharks that they sent a helicopter out to warn us. Ever try to hear something in a howling windstorm from a guy in a helicopter rotating above you? But, I figured something was wrong and headed in...to be met by the press, which I avoided and went home. My wife read about the shark deal in *USA Today* the next day and wondered if I had been out. I lied.

The way I got to go to the parties put on by the NFL and the media...ESPN especially...was through a bad misunderstanding. One of their executives must have misunderstood something I said and thought I was the head of marketing of a major corporation...a pure misunderstanding on his part. I have no idea how he came to be so misinformed. He got me credentials and they kept getting renewed year after year. I made friends with a group of people who after a while knew me... and I was golden. And, the NFL knows how to party.

I met everyone...coaches, players, wives, girlfriends, wives and girlfriends, girlfriends for rent, suits from the league, media people and announcers. I also met all the "hangers-on"...who am I kidding, I was a hanger-on.

One of the hangers-on was MC Hammer. MC Hammer was a rapper who was popular ("U Can't Touch This") for a while and had or has the best-selling rap album of all time. He was a brilliant performer. He was not a brilliant businessman. He was at a party with me and bragged that he had flown his private jet over to go to this one party and then had to head back to, I think, New York. The next night his fighter was fighting in, maybe, Madison Square Garden. He told me he had sunk a lot of money into the kid and planned to sell his interest right after the fight. I think the kid he got rid of was a young Mike Tyson...whoops, missed out on that one. MC Hammer got rich overnight and poor overnight...but I've got to say he was fun to be around and full of electricity and had a line of bullshit a mile long. My kind of guy.

Deion Sanders provided a great laugh for me. He was big time...a two-sport star...good looking...great on camera...always had something to say...the press loved him...ego and all. ESPN set him up one time. Two huge ex-NFL lineman types were doing a live interview with Deion and they had rigged up a huge rat on a string that they pulled across his feet during the interview. He went out of his mind...great television. Apparently, Deion did not like rats.

The Pro Bowl was always lame. No one tried. I take that back, one guy tried. I went to the last game that Mike Singletary would ever play...the 1993 Pro Bowl. Two teams going three-quarter speed and Mike playing like he always played...all out. Mike and I attended the same church and lived near one another...I followed his whole career. So damn proud of him

When I say it was lame...it was lame. It was that same year, 1993, when quarterback Troy Aikman left the game and went to the airport without even telling the coach. Can you imagine? Players would also come over and talk to their friends in the stands during the game...which was fun for guys like me, not so fun for the coaches trying to get them into the game. But the Pro Bowl gave me an excellent excuse to go surfing in Hawaii for 14 great years and kept me semi-sane. Fun times indeed.

Just have to mention one more NFL player...but not by name...he is bigger than me...might be offended by this and I might see him sometime. So...

I became friendly with an NFL great. He told me that I should come see his place. I traveled all the time and ended up one day near his house. I called him and he invited me out. I believe he had the biggest house I have ever seen...just plain gigantic.

In the back of the house was a lake that covered several acres...that is, decent sized, but not a big lake...it is a small lake. In the lake, a huge yacht...huge...like an ocean-going yacht. He told me we would have lunch on the yacht. We did. He had a captain for this yacht and the captain was given instructions to weigh anchor... and we were off. We were off on a dizzying number of very tight circles around this pitiful lake...in his very serious yacht. If you are curious who this football star is, you can easily find him by doing an internet search for "people who have WAY too much money."

I'm not completely selfish. Some years I would take a second Hawaiian vacation and actually bring along the family. On one of these I had the bright idea of taking my family out to another place on Oahu quite famous for not warmly welcoming visitors. We were not warmly welcomed in our all-white tourist rental car...not welcomed at all. In fact, a giant guy in a beer delivery truck gave my wife and me and my two young children the finger and then proceeded to swerve his truck into us, pinning our car in against the weeds on the side of the road. He then got out of his truck with a baseball bat and made it clear he was going to beat me to a pulp...for reasons unknown. I told the kids to duck, that I was probably going to kill this guy, and I floored the car and ran it straight at him. I have no idea how he got out of the way and I did not stick around to find out why he was so angry. Trust me, he had me so concerned for my own and my family's safety that I fully expected to hit him with my car and run him over with both axles. It was him or us. He got lucky...and I guess I did, too.

That afternoon, on the way home, I had to drive through that same area. I was just a little nervous. It started to rain...hard. And then I heard a noise and felt the car jerking around. One of the tires on the rental had blown out. This was not a place I wanted to stop and change a tire in the driving rain, so I probably drove 15 miles on that completely flat tire on the freeway at pretty good speed. I pulled into a tire shop and everyone in the shop came running out to see why my left rear tire was on fire. They put out the fire with an extinguisher and we all looked at the one ribbon of rubber left on the totally-flattened rim and I asked, "Well, boys, do you think you can throw a patch on that so I can get it back to Avis?" Best laugh of the trip.

CHAPTER FORTY

Taking My 80-Something-Year-Old Parents to Hawaii

I think it was their 60th wedding anniversary when I took my parents to Hawaii. I told them I would fly them over with Linda and me, first class, get a suite at the Hawaiian Princess Resort (the pink hotel on Waikiki), take them to the other islands and accompany them to see anything they wanted to see, including Pearl Harbor. I would pay every penny, but there were two quid pro quos. First, they both had to get new bathing suits and leave the ones they normally wore, the ones they had apparently bought when they were in high school, at home. Second, they had to go snorkeling with me once and Linda and I would see to their safety. They agreed.

When you are 80-something and a full-figured woman who had always been a stunner but was now 80-something, buying a new bathing suit could be traumatic. So Mom took Dad with her to Nordstrom to try on suits. It would take a book to describe my dad. Let's just say he was direct and could be a bit cruel...sound familiar?

The saleslady at Nordstrom figures out the dynamic with my mom instantly. She does everything she can to make this a pleasant experience for her. Dad waits outside the changing room. Out come Mom and the saleslady, with Mom in bathing suit option number one. Mom is pretty much horrified at this point but determined to get this done. The salesperson asks my dad what he likes most about the suit. His answer: "I like the way the straps disappear into the fat on her shoulders."

Yup...lucky I ever got them to Hawaii.

They did make it to Hawaii and we had a ball. I took them snorkeling at Hanauma Bay. Mom gave it a minor try, but it was kind of scary for her, so I let her off the hook. Dad loved it. He clung to me like a barnacle and I dragged him all over the bay. Lots of fun with my dad, who was in his mid 80s at the time.

We also traveled to the Big Island and I hiked them a short distance out to the running lava. That was pretty amazing. Back on Oahu, we met with some old neighbors from California who now lived in Hawaii, and we loved our time with them. Dad asked who else I knew on that island and I named several others I had grown up with in Palos Verdes. I also mentioned that there was an old friend on Oahu whom I had never been able to find or reach, but I knew for sure he was there...and they knew him from my youth...Steve Maier. One hour later, while we were in an art gallery on Waikiki, my dad comes over to me and points to a man, saying..."I think that is Steve." I went over to him and...it was. Back in touch with a guy I love, and I now get to see him all the time...thanks, Dad.

Hawaii has been in just about every year of our marriage of over 50 years, with Linda's grandparents living here for many decades before we ever set foot on the islands. It is our forever home now. I am thankful for the memories, adventures and good friends I have here. I love Hawaii.

CHAPTER FORTY-ONE

Linda's Mink Coat

You might be able to discern the flow of history from the stories I am telling. Some occurred long ago, in a land not "woke." I don't say that in a derogatory way, in a lot of ways I think a woke land is a better land, but maybe not always. Case in point…mink coats. Today I would be the first to stand in line to say I think the idea of an actual mink coat is barbaric. However, that has not always been the case. At one time I thought they were a sign of class and wealth and beautiful and necessary if you lived in a cold climate.

Our family had lived in Southern California for all of our lives. When the kids were young and Linda and I were in our early thirties, I got transferred from Southern California to Chicago, Illinois. This was a culture and a lifestyle shock that lasted, in one form or another, for something like 24 years, until I could retire and move to Hawaii.

I know this is hard to believe, but I had never seen snow fall until I was close to 30. I had been in snow in the mountains around Los Angeles, but only after it had snowed, and the roads were cleared. I had not ever seen snow drift down out of the sky. Chicago put an end to that good run.

My career depended on me being able to do a good job at work and make my kids and wife happy at home. I would love to tell you that family was so much more important to me than career, but that would just not be true. They were almost equally important to me…horrible as that sounds. So, I tried hard to make the whole thing work out for all of us…with some success and a few failures.

We were just a bit freaked out about moving to Chicago. I actually thought it was possibly life-threatening. I did not understand cold, or ice, or wind, or lightning, or hail. Tornadoes were a complete mystery to me. We had no winter clothes. We really did not know how to prepare.

So we bought a house big enough that we could live inside it forever if necessary. The basement...people do not have basements in California...had a running track, a karate mat, an area for stretching, a nine-station Universal weightlifting machine such as you might find at a top gym in those days, stereo, TV, ping pong table and a place for our pet rabbit. It was so unique that a neighbor, NFL great Walter Payton, came over to see it and was pretty impressed.

I also did not know how to drive in snow. We had two small Honda Civics. First time it snowed they spun around like toys on the ice and slush. I got rid of them immediately and put some good old-fashioned American iron around me... with front-wheel drive, which was good in the snow.

I had moved Linda and the kids to Illinois in time to get the kids enrolled for the start of the school year. I had an office to run and close in California, so I stayed until just before Christmas. On Christmas Eve, I was back in Chicago in the new home, ready to enjoy our first Chicago Christmas. And it turned out to be a spectacular Christmas.

I arranged for tickets to The Nutcracker at McCormick Place in downtown Chicago...Christmas Eve. We went to the afternoon performance that got out about dinner time. We then went to the landmark Berghoff, a wonderful German restaurant, for an early dinner. It was perfect.

When we finished dinner, we walked outside, and it was snowing. This was the kind of snow you only get a few times a year in Chicago, giant flakes kind of floating down gently, making the whole scene look like an animation...absolutely beautiful. We decided to bundle up and walk down Miracle Mile to see all the window decorations—and they were also spectacular. It was now getting into the evening on Christmas Eve, so basically no stores were open...except one.

We looked down the block and I saw a store selling furs with a neon sign flashing to indicate it was open. I suggested we speed up and go in to see what fur coats actually looked like. My mom had a fur coat that Dad had bought her in Asbury Park, New Jersey, right before he went off to Europe to fight in World War ll. It was beaver and it looked like the beaver had had a hard life. That was the only fur coat I had ever seen in person...they were not standard fare in California or in my social circles, as we were not the rich and famous.

The salesman was delighted to see us...or anyone for that matter...business was a little slow with everyone now home for Christmas Eve. I asked if he would mind letting my beautiful wife try on a coat or two. Not at all...it would be his pleasure.

Linda is a blond and he started with a white coyote coat...sounds horrible, but it was really quite lovely and warm. However, it blended in with her hair color and did not pop in any way. What else you got?

Next up, a fox coat...pretty much red in color...looked nice, but there was something about it neither of us liked. Nope, that would not do.

I asked him about a mink coat...weren't they black and wouldn't that look nice on my blond wife? He smiled and in a very professional and nice way said that it certainly would, but that I had made it clear I was on a budget and his mink coats were not budget items...perhaps I would like to see a rabbit coat?

Well, we sure as hell did not want to see a rabbit coat, we had rabbits for pets... they were like family. Back to the minks...what did he have that I might be able to afford? Well, he had a mink stole...kind of a cape-looking thing...the feel and warmth of fur, but much more affordable. Took one look...no thanks.

So, this gambit was going nowhere. The kids were ready to go...20 minutes ago. Linda was not having fun...in fact it was kind of frustrating. Neither of us really knew what to expect or the right questions to ask or the cost of anything and these were expensive enough that it really would not be wise to make a hasty decision. So, as much as I wanted to delight my wife on our first Christmas Eve in Chicago, this was all coming to a crashing halt.

I thanked the nice man and told him I appreciated his time and expertise. We gathered up our things and I tried to think of something that we might do on the way to the car to end our downtown Christmas experience on a high note. But as we were ready to go, the salesman said, "Sir, you would be doing your beautiful wife a disservice if you didn't at least let her try on a full-length Blackglama (apparently a very good brand in those days) mink coat. He said he had one in solid black that was exactly her size and he would be right back with it. He also said that it was out of my price range and he just wanted us to see it for future reference. What the heck...bring it on.

It may be hard for you to relate to decades-old sensibilities and style, but I can tell you that when he brought out that beautiful full-length solid black, softly shining Blackglama mink coat...my heart about stopped. He put it on Linda, and she lit up like a Christmas tree. Linda has the world's greatest teeth and you could see every one of them...she was smiling like I had never before seen.

Linda twirled around like she was a game show hostess. She looked at herself in the mirror, trying every angle she could find. The kids actually applauded.

Well, all of this had put me in a difficult position. I had kind of let the genie out of the bottle and it was now up to me to shove that genie right back in...and the damn salesman was no help...he too was applauding and pretending to wipe tears out of his eyes. I was screwed...unless I was quick and clever. And I was every bit of that.

I asked Linda if she liked the lining of the coat...which was maybe silk and beautiful. She said that she could care less about the lining of the coat...that the coat itself made her feel like magic. I said...well, if we are even going to consider something as expensive as this, you would have to be in love with every part of it... give the lining an inspection and see what you think.

At that, Linda opened up the coat and looked at the lining. In beautiful white thread, her name was stitched into the lining in a perfect cursive signature that looked much like her actual signature, because it was. I had set up the whole thing... got them the signature...selected the coat...worked out the timing and the sales show with the salesman and paid for the coat in full before we ever set foot in the store. This was her coat.

I can tell you...this was a BIG hit. As you can tell from my writings in this book and others, I don't spend a lot of time trying to look smart or good...mainly because the opposite is often the case...and those stories are the most interesting. But I wrote this one for you to show you I can bring it when I need to. I was on my A game that night and it was just as she described it...magic.

We floated out of there...didn't even need a box because Linda was wearing the mink. She looked like a million dollars. The kids and I looked good just by being with her. We all kind of floated down Miracle Mile to our car, quarter-sized snowflakes floating in the still cold air and landing on our smiling faces. A Christmas to remember.

CHAPTER FORTY-TWO

Getting Braces on My Teeth at Age 70

Like Soupy Sales once said, "Be true to your teeth or they will be false to you."

At about age 69, my teeth brought me to decision time. I'd gotten whacked in the mouth a couple of times over the years by surfboards...that did my teeth no good at all. I'd bathed them in sugar all day long for about seven decades. That turned out not to be optimal for good dental health either. Truth told, the teeth were not that good-looking to begin with and I had SO much dental work done over the years that it all got problematic. I finally lost a tooth in the back, to go along with the four front ones I lost in my teens from a surfboard to the mouth and our family decision (read...we did not have the money) to have them fixed, just yank them out and put in a bridge. By the way, that bridge looked far better than my original teeth and lasted 50 years...so, thank you Mr. Dentist whose name is lost in history and who is probably long dead.

As I said, decision time. Get 'em fixed or start to lose them one by one. I chose to get them fixed...properly.

There is an amazing dentist in Honolulu named Dr. Jon Yoshimura. I had several dentist friends mention him as THE go-to guy for the work I needed done. My first visit for his evaluation was three and a half hours long. Think about that... three and one-half hours just to figure out what would need to be done. Turns out that what needed to be done was...everything. And, it would cost a fortune. By fortune I mean...next time you hear some Hollywood type talking about how much their cosmetic surgery cost...I have them beat. Not all the money was going to Dr. Yoshimura; much of it going to various other dental specialists on his virtual team. And, the work would take over two years to complete...with me flying back and forth to Honolulu from Kona and no insurance helping to pay for any of this. Vanity has a price.

By the way, it was not just me. I had Linda come over for her evaluation, thinking maybe we could get a small group discount of some kind. Her evaluation took ten minutes...ten. Said she had the best teeth he had ever seen. Bit of a contrast to my damn situation.

So, a year into this ordeal, the various doctors had performed miracles and things were looking good...to me. Not to Dr. Yoshimura. He noted that my bottom teeth were crooked. Yeah...so what? Well, I had spent all this money to get my mouth back together, shouldn't it all look good cosmetically? Also, there was some technical thing about my bite that needed to be corrected or the work already done would not last. So, off I went to see an orthodontist.

I had managed to avoid braces for nearly 70 years. I ended up getting a full bottom set of old-style metal, pointy, shiny, food gathering braces. Had them on for over a year. Straightened out my teeth and made the extensive dental work come together nicely. I can now actually smile without people turning their heads and can gnaw through drywall and rebar with the new caps and bridge and implants, should I ever be trapped in a collapsed building.

Along the way, the braces thing was a humbling experience. I would go into the orthodontist's office every so often and sit outside in the waiting room in the small chairs there, surrounded by fidgety children with fucked-up mouths, all of us waiting to see the orthodontist. I was often asked if I had brought my grandchild in...I would smile. They asked no more.

Linda decided not to be outdone. She decided to correct an emerging bite problem before it became a problem, a concept unheard of on my side of the family. She got invisible braces on her whole mouth.

So, off we go to Europe with our 12-year-old granddaughter. Young Ava has on braces. Linda has on braces. Old Donny has on braces. We were quite the crew.

Got to say, so glad I got the work done and got it done by the best team out there. Worth every penny...and there were lots of pennies. I did exact one bit of getting even from Dr. Yoshimura...I paid a large amount of the bill in cash. Linda and I escorted him to the bank to safely deposit it. Along the way, I used an old magic move (I once studied magic...never was very good at it) to distract him and swap the bags the money was in...as in, the money was no longer in the bag he was carrying to the bank. When he proudly went to pour out the cash for deposit, a single dollar bill came floating out. That was the only serious fun I had during the whole two-year dental re-build, with the exception of the last day and my first look in the mirror at the best-looking set of actually working teeth I had had in my whole life.

I do not focus on points in the stories in this book, but this one has a point. If you have a medical, mental or dental problem and have decided that you will just let your eventual death solve that problem for you...think again. It was tough doing all that dental work the right way, but worth every moment of it...and worth every dollar, including the one floating out of his huge bag of money at the bank. Thank you, Dr. Jon Yoshimura and Rae and Karin and everyone on his team and his virtual team. Best in the business.

CHAPTER FORTY-THREE

Two Bullets in China

Linda and I went to China in November 2019. Our first trip to China and we got to see quite a bit...from Beijing to the Great Wall, the Terracotta Army, Yangtze River, panda bears, Shanghai...and to take several plane rides and a multi-day cruise on the river. The size and scale of the country is amazing. It is organized, growing like crazy, modern with great protection of the ancient sites, clean, busy and beautiful. We were there when the smog was not...the skies were blue and the temperatures were cool, but not cold. We loved our trip and felt safe at all times... even though we were not!

One highlight was a short trip from downtown Shanghai to the airport via a bullet train. It travelled at nearly 270 miles an hour in complete comfort. We loved it. That was bullet number one for us.

Bullet number two we never saw coming. Our itinerary said we would leave the Yangtze River cruise on November 13 and visit the city of Wuhan. The night before we were offered a trip into the wet market...which we, thankfully, declined. On the 13th, with no warning, our plans were changed to take us to an airport more than 100 miles from Wuhan where we would then fly to Shanghai. At the airport we noticed a large machine that we had to pass under...a machine we could see was reading our body temperatures. To the side, a doctor and nurse in protective clothing were ready to pull those not passing the temperature check into a room for further testing.

Given that the Chinese government told the world in December 2019 that they had identified the COVID-19 virus in Wuhan, we feel very fortunate to have just missed being exposed. Our travel agency or the Chinese government and/or

God or just plain good luck kept us out of the most dangerous health spot on earth at the most dangerous time. Whatever the combination of good fortune, we are thankful.

And we are thankful that we visited China. In a world filled with problems, they have found many innovative solutions to resolve some important issues... while still struggling to address others. We found China to be much more than we expected, flawed in ways that Americans would not like...such as censorship and one-party control...and powerful beyond belief. They are a force to be reckoned with today and tomorrow.

CHAPTER FORTY-FOUR

A Life That Matters

Long ago and far away, the 1968 Olympics took place in Mexico City. The track and field participants were people I knew, people I had competed against, people who had beaten me into dust at each encounter. They were my competitors and, in many instances, my friends. That 1968 U.S. Track and Field Team was arguably the greatest track and field team ever assembled.

But the games were not without controversy. Two U.S. runners, Tommie Smith and John Carlos, came in first and third in the 200-meter dash. They are both black. The silver medal went to a white Australian, Peter Norman. Tommie and John decided to make a stand for black America, to wear a black glove on one hand, thrust that black glove into the air and bow their heads as the Star Spangled Banner played with them on the victory podium. Peter joined them symbolically by wearing a button that supported their cause.

A little personal history...

I was raised in an all-white area of Los Angeles and I'm white. Most of the area that we lived in was affluent, although we were not. I was a sprinter/hurdler/long jumper...all three of those events were dominated by black runners and jumpers in those days, with some very notable exceptions.

So, when I competed, and especially when I went off to college, the people I travelled with and hung out with and competed against looked much more like America than the wonderful, but monochromatic, community I was fortunate to grow up in. My new environment was stimulating, interesting and filled with new challenges. And those new connections to the world were eye-opening indeed.

By my junior year in college, I had learned what hatred looked like...from both sides of the fence. I saw how black folks were treated and it was not pretty. I briefly dated a young lady in Compton and the way I was treated driving into and out of that community was not pretty. There was one hell of a divide amongst the people...then and now.

A lot of the world did not understand the "disrespect" for America shown by Tommie and John. Those two were thrown off the team. Peter was treated no better when he returned to Australia. He was basically erased from Australian sports and his accomplishments meant nothing...he had embarrassed the Australian people.

And a bit more on Peter...his feeling was that all people are equal and he supported that equality. He also did not like the way that the Aboriginal people of Australia had been treated and he mentioned that history. Good-bye to his brief stay in the public eye...he was done. How dare he bring that up?

I had been around Tommie and John...raced Tommie's brother, but could not even qualify to carry dirty track shoes for either Tommie or John. I was good. They were supermen. I have never seen such speed. I did not get to talk much with Tommie after the Olympics, but I did see John Carlos at track meets and had meaningful conversations with him. He suffered after the Olympics...his stand cost him and Tommie dearly.

My junior year in college I had a track coach named Steve Simmons. Coach Simmons was only a few years older than I and had been a hurdler and sprinter at Chapman University. He took a real interest in me and several others...in particular, Doug Eckert and Bing Howell. Doug was the son of wealthy parents from my home town and one of my best friends in the world. Bing came from Jamaica and was new to America. Doug and Bing were both scholar/athletes. I was more an athlete...end of story. Doug and I were white. Bing and Coach were black.

Coach would kid Doug and me about where we were raised and our upbringing. He would get mad at me when I kidded Bing about his Jamaican background...and Bing would get boiling mad. But, at the end of the day, we were all part of one team and we loved one another...and I do not use that word lightly...we cared deeply about one another and stood for each other's successes.

Coach Simmons was stern and tough and scary. He worked us hard. You really would not want to cross him. I remember refusing to run an event at the end of a very long day at the NCAA Division II Regionals in San Francisco. Coach told me Bing was injured and I needed to fill in for him on the 4x400 meter relay. I had already run heats and finals in three or four other events that day and had a handful of NCAA medals...and I hate the 400-meter. I told him no. That did not sit well. I believe he beat me with my own spikes and changed my mind. I ran...poorly...but we earned yet another medal and points for our team. Maybe not the kind of motivational leadership you might approve of today, but it sure as hell motivated me and I have one more NCAA medal than I would have if he had let my refusal stand.

Coach introduced us to people. He made sure we saw what it was like being black in America. We learned about civil rights activist Harry Edwards and the Black Power movement...not because he was teaching us that stuff, but because he got us interested in expanding our own horizons.

After the NCAA Division II Finals in Ashland, Ohio, in 1969, Coach took our outstanding high jumper (and my senior year roommate), Jim Frost, and me with him to stay with his parents in Dayton, Ohio. The part of the city he lived in was about 100% black. We were not. One afternoon he took us to a local bar. We got seated and he quietly moved to the other side of the room. When our eyes adjusted to the dark, Jim and I realized that we were the only two white guys in the bar...maybe ever. One of the patrons moved his chair right next to mine and asked what we were doing in HIS bar. I pointed to Coach and said, "We're with him." The guy bellowed across the bar at Coach, "Are these two white boys with you?" Coach spoke right up..."Never saw them in my life." Uh-oh. At that, the whole bar exploded in laughter...Coach had set us up.

I guess why I bring all this up is to say...I found it enlightening to see things from the point of view of others...still do. I'm not here to lecture anyone on race relations. I'm just here to say that the divide existed then, exists today and seems to me to be a self-inflicted wound on humanity. I am last in line to approve violence or hate talk or rioting or mayhem...but I am also quick to say...I get it...I understand that enough is enough and it is time to put this divide behind us forever. Less happy talk. More action...faster. And would it not be wonderful if we could find a way to do this out of love and respect for one another rather than hate and retribution? OK, that is asking too much. But listening to one another...really listening...being open to change...helping rather than defending...treating each other with respect... that is not too much to ask...is it?

So, what brings me to that conclusion? Coach Simmons, Tommie Smith and John Carlos...they bring me to that conclusion. Coach Simmons eventually became a manager on the U.S. Olympic Track Team...head manager for the 1980 and 1984 teams and Team Leader for the 1992 U.S. Olympic Track Team in Barcelona. Prior to those assignments, he coached Olympic athletes from Africa, South America and India. He also had a long-time involvement with our Decathlon Team. He was a manger of the U.S. World Track and Field Team...and Linda and I accompanied him to Sweden for that event. He became a respected leader...and is to this day... among U.S. and world track coaches.

And the world changed for Tommie Smith and John Carlos. People began to understand their stand and embrace their actions. There is a bronze statue honoring them on the campus of San Jose University in California. They are both sought-after speakers. Life is now good for them.

Peter Norman had a similar change in his life. However, it was hard to come by. Even when the Olympics came to Australia, he was left out. Finally, late in his life, he was beginning to get the kind of respect he deserved.

When Coach Simmons heard that Peter Norman was not invited to the 2000 Olympics in Australia, he got the money together and paid for transportation for Peter and his wife and then gave up his own bed at a hotel so they would have a place to stay. Coach Simmons slept on the floor in another coach's room in the Olympic Village. The U.S. team rallied around Peter Norman and showed him the respect he deserved and let him know exactly how much they appreciated his support and sacrifice.

The Peter Norman story is too good to just mention in passing. So, with permission, I am including this article written by Greg Baum in *The Age*, an Australian newspaper, on October 11, 2006. Here is that article, including Australian spelling and use of words we might never encounter...I think you will enjoy it.

Athletes' final salute to an Australian great
By Greg Baum
Published in *The Age* on October 11, 2006
Re-printed with permission

John Carlos ran for the US in the Mexico City Olympics, but he could not have swum for his country then; he would not have been allowed into a swimming club. It was 1968, and America's black people had had enough.

"We still had lack of employment, lack of quality housing, lack of education, lack of opportunity," Carlos said yesterday. "There were insults, humiliation, indignities, just because of the colour of our skin."

Sport was only part-refuge. "Someone had to take a stance. It was wrong, just wrong."

Carlos, from Harlem, and Tommie Smith, from California, became standard-bearers for the Olympic Project for Human Rights. Among their ideas was to boycott the 1968 Games. For even mooting this, they received death threats. Carlos said he was unfazed. "If God wanted me to die for what I believe in, I was ready to die. The point is that you can kill me, but you can't kill my belief," he said.

Carlos and Smith were chosen for the Olympic team that US track and field official Steve Simmons yesterday said was the greatest American sports team.

At the Games, the black athletes met often to discuss how they might take their cause to the world. It would not be easy. Carlos and Smith agreed they had to make their stance on the dais.

Into this fraught atmosphere, as all have been reminded this week, walked Peter Norman, a Melburnian. In the 200-metres final, he split Smith and Carlos, winning silver. As they waited for the presentation ceremony, the Americans asked Norman if he would join their protest. Norman was from a Salvation Army family. The slogan on the back of his training tracksuit read: "Jesus Saves". In a way, he was like them, an evangelist. He agreed.

Carlos had left behind a pair of black gloves he planned to wear, but Smith had his, and at Norman's suggestion, they wore one each. All were afraid. Norman wore Carlos' OPHR rights badge.

The image of the three on the dais, heads bowed, the Americans delivering the "Black Salute", is regarded one of the most powerful of the 20th century.

Lasting repercussions followed. Smith and Carlos were dropped from the relays and the team. Oppobrium ensued at home. Friends deserted, money became scarce, more threats came. Norman paid a price, too. "It tore up all our first marriages," Carlos said. His wife committed suicide.

But history would show their gesture was not in vain. Norman could not have grasped how his part would resonate.

"Peter Norman resurrected my faith in the human race, white folks included," Carlos said. "He let me know that all white people was not like what I saw in the US." Smith said Norman was not just a great athlete, but a great humanitarian.

In the '90s, Norman visited Smith in the US. They talked for four days. "He was not a man without his troubles," Smith said.

Simmons helped fund the telemovie *Fist of Freedom*. It won an Emmy. At the 2000 Sydney Olympics, Simmons was aghast to read that Norman — "the greatest sprinter in the hemisphere" — had been asked to play a peripheral role.

When a stranger accidentally nudged Simmons as he read, he turned and hit him, such was his fury. Simmons put Norman and his wife, Jan, on a plane to Sydney, and he bunked in with the US track coach so the Normans could have his hotel room.

Norman went to introduce himself to US Olympic hurdler Edwin Moses, but Moses replied: "I know who you are". That night, at Michael Johnson's birthday party, Johnson came up to say: "You're my hero."

In the taxi home, Norman said to Simmons: "I didn't know anybody cared so much". Replied Simmons: "We do care, and we always will". He had become an honorary American.

Smith said he once asked Norman why he was not bitter towards Australia for neglecting him. "I have a love of all men because I believe we're all going to the same place," he replied.

Last year, San Jose State University erected a statue depicting the 1968 podium. Norman was not part of the statue. Smith said the exclusion did not bother Norman. "I was only a pebble thrown into deep, still waters," he said to Smith. "My hope was that the ripples would reach the shore of love."

In Australia, Norman's nephew, Matt, thought it a travesty that even here, Norman was only known as "the white guy" in the 1968 image. He has spent the past four years making the movie, Salute. Norman was to go the Los Angeles at the end of October for the promotions, and was excited. But last week he had a heart attack and died.

The US track and field body proclaimed last Monday, the day of Norman's funeral, "Peter Norman Day", an honour unprecedented in its 170-year history. Smith and Carlos came to Australia to be pallbearers.

At 38 years' distance, it is easy to overlook the importance of what they did, and the courage it took. Smith said he regularly met young athletes who vaguely knew his story, but presumed him to be dead. Yesterday, that looked to be a greatly exaggerated idea.

Cathy Freeman followed in the footsteps of the trio when she defied orders to not carry the Aboriginal flag at presentations. But otherwise, black athletes are less given to grand gestures now. Perhaps it is because they are more equal. If so, they can thank Smith, Carlos and the late, fondly remembered Norman.

Thank you to Greg Baum and *The Age* for allowing me to re-produce that article.

So, when Peter Norman died, Coach Simmons got Tommie Smith and John Carlos together, rounded up transportation for them and the three flew to Australia for Peter Norman's funeral. At the funeral, Tommie Smith and John Carlos...two strong, American, proud, competitive black men, carried their rival...

their friend...an Australian white guy who felt that equality was as important as they felt it was...to the finish line. I tear up every time I think of their actions.

So...lives matter. I'm thankful for Coach Simmons' life...he matters. He sure as heck matters to me. And I also hope that all of us can find a way to act with care, concern, understanding and love toward one another. If we do, we matter too.

CHAPTER FORTY-FIVE

COVID-19...The Pandemic...and Being Locked Down

After reading this much of the book, do you think I am the kind of guy who would do well in a lockdown? Well, let me surprise you. First, I had no idea this thing would last so long or be so devasting. Linda and I could see we were in the high-risk group, so we have taken the pandemic (it is still under way as I write this in late 2020) completely seriously and protected ourselves and others from ourselves. We have not been out much. We pay to have our groceries delivered. We have been out to eat one time in the last five months and that was outdoor dining. We have only been on one plane in five months, to go to Oahu for an annual dental check-up with our great dentist, in his office that now looks like an operating room from the TV show *M*A*S*H*. Our gallery business has been mostly closed for months. This is one strange time.

However, we made a decision early on, let's use this time effectively. We thought then...may not quite be feeling that way now...that we might never get a lockdown time like this again in our lifetime. Time to look at the things on the "To Do" list that we never get done...and do them. But first, we decided to put our physical selves on a much improved cardio and workout plan and routinize (if that is a word) things like daily vitamin intake and dental hygiene and other practices that, if actually done every single day, might help us to live a week or two longer in the long run. And, we have done a pretty good job at all of the above.

Once we worked through the old items on the To Do list, I turned to my writing. I write fast...really fast...always have. I banged out *What's Left of Don* in a week or so. It then took me several months to get it edited (actually my fabulous editor, Tanya Lee, edited that book in about one week), have the cover designed,

153

get the interior layout done, get a donhurzeler.com website up and running, plan my marketing, have Dan Snow get it ready for Kindle and Amazon and pump that book out the door to a great reception on July 4, 2020. My publishing company, which I love...oh, and which I own...Kua Bay Publishing LLC, and the smarts, arms, legs and minds behind that company, Steve Bennett and Authorbytes, got the book done in record time.

Then, damn, I started thinking of all the stories I did not have room for in that first *What's Left of Don*. As I started to organize those stories I realized they were as good as, or better...and quite different...from the stories I had already told. So, I sat down to write this book. Took me another week to write it. Toward the end, it became a race.

My great next-door neighbor, Doug Reynolds, has a brand-new house. He had a mountain of rock delivered to his driveway. I asked him who was going to move that for him and spread it where he needed it in his yard...twelve cubic yards of gravel-sized rock. He said he was going to do it himself with a shovel, wheelbarrow and bucket. I told him I had 30,000 words written on this new book, aiming for about 55,000 words at completion. I told him I would be done before he was. The race was on. He worked that mountain down to a small hill before the rain got him last night. I know he will be up early to finish his job and claim the bragging rights. TOO LATE, DOUG...I got up at 2 a.m. and will be done well before the sun comes up. Oh, I love competition.

That was not the end of our COVID optimization. Linda came up with a character that is cute as heck and she will use it on decorated items or on things like COVID-19 masks. She is an excellent artist and the character is quite commercial. May even find its way into the book or onto our donhurzeler.com website.

Then I got an email from God in a dream. This has never happened to me before. I woke up from the dream and realized that I had what I think is a blockbuster story line for a novel, delivered to me in complete detail throughout the full arc of the story...from start to finish. I got up and started typing and 13.5 hours later had a complete outline and much of the detail of that book completed. I have it out for comment right now. Once I get that back I will find out if I can write dialog and master character development...something I have little experience with...but I will give it my best and get help if and when I get stuck. I have five books out the door already and a coffee table book of photographs taken by myself, my wife and two partners and I would love to add a novel to the list...so more to do in lockdown.

Linda and I also came up with an idea to expand our professional photo business...make a huge step forward online. So, we have been trademarking, incorporating, grabbing domain names and contacting infrastructure and online marketing people to make this thing happen. Pretty exciting.

All that sounds pretty good for an old guy of 73. Trust me, I would rather be back in our old routine...going to the beach with friends, traveling the world on crowded airplanes, working in our beautiful photo gallery and welcoming visitors to our island. I have just about had it with the lockdown...I am hoping that is well behind all of us by the time you have read this book. If not, I may start taking online classes to keep me busy. Please, God, save me from that.

CHAPTER FORTY-SIX

Conclusion...There is No Conclusion

There is no conclusion, at least not right now. There is "continuing" and there will eventually be "dead," but right now, no conclusion. I plan to continue my quirky and uncareful life for as long as I can and then I will do my best to get out of the way for others to have all the fun. In the meantime...what a life...I am thankful for my life.. down to the last atom at the bottom of my feet.

And thanks for taking the time to share parts of this journey with me. Aloha.

"To succeed in life, you need three things...a wishbone, a backbone and a funny bone." —Reba McEntire

ACKNOWLEDGEMENTS

I mentioned my wife, Linda, as always being a partner for me in my writing... and she certainly was this time around. Tanya Lee edited this book and did her normal quick and careful job, while also keeping me from sharing a few stories that did not need to be shared. I appreciate both Linda and Tanya for their help and encouragement.

Special acknowledgment goes to Steve Bennett of Authorbytes. He and his team are the workhorses behind the publishing company that published this book...the prestigious Kua Bay Publishing LLC. I say "prestigious" because I own the company and I am shameless. But Steve is so much more than a workhorse. In the true sense of the word, he is my muse. He is so creative...thinks in such different ways than I do...that a simple phone conversation with him might change a whole project or challenge me to think very differently about certain portions of the project. I almost always hang up the phone after speaking to him and think, "Son of a gun...never thought of that in my life and I think he is right." So...I just want Steve to know that he is very much appreciated and respected by me.

ABOUT THE AUTHOR

Don Hurzeler was an athlete in his youth, a surfer all of his life, a man of the sea, a runner, photographer, writer and a successful businessman. He values his wife, son, daughter, grandchildren and his other relatives more each day. He misses his mom and dad and sister and grandparents and assorted aunts and uncles, coaches and friends...people who have already told their stories and headed off to whatever comes next. His friends are his friends for life, and he loves them. Don now lives with Linda in Kailua-Kona, Hawaii, where he will stay until he has finished his work, his play and his much enjoyed naps. Don also finds it hard to write in a manner that makes it look like someone else is writing this about him, so he will quit right here.

Other Books by the Author

Designated for Success...a book for insurance professionals available as an eBook on Amazon.com or email the author for one of the few remaining hard copies...out of print.

The Way Up: How to Keep Your Career Moving in the Right Direction...a book for people in corporate America who will need to learn how to handle both success and failure, as they will surely experience both. Good insights on what it takes to succeed. Available as an eBook on Amazon.com or write the author for one of the few remaining hard copies...out of print.

Smells Like Retirement...a book about figuring out who you will be, what you will do and where you will do it in your retirement. A must-read book for anyone getting ready to retire or recently retired. Available as a paperback on Amazon and an eBook on Amazon.com

What's Left of Don...a memoir filled with stories and laughter, designed to either make you feel better about your own life decisions or to challenge you to get even more out of your life. Available as both a paperback on Amazon and an eBook on Amazon.com

The Hawaiian Collection...a coffee table book of fine art photographs taken by Don and Linda Hurzeler and their partners, C.J. Kale and Nick Selway. Write the author for details.

How to Contact the Author

Don can be reached at djhzz@aol.com or from the Contact page on his website at donhurzeler.com

Check out Don's website at donhurzeler.com

The Cover Photo

I took this photo of a leaping wildebeest at the Mara River crossing in Tanzania. Many people have commented that it looks more like a painting than a photo, but it is indeed a photo and it is not doctored up. The photo looks very much as the scene looked in person.

I am a professional photographer, so I did not just stumble upon this scene. We planned for it and ended up at the right place at the right time with the right people around us. Thomson Safaris planned and conducted the excursion for us, in partnership with Nature's Best Photography magazine. We had an executive from the African Wildlife Foundation with us, Craig Sholley. We also had one of the world's great photographers with us, Jeff Vanuga. Additionally, we had guides from Thomson Safaris who knew how to get us in position in case the river crossing took place. And then...it took place.

The crossing happens when wildebeests by the hundreds of thousands, along with a large number of zebras, all decide to get to the other side of the Mara River to find better food and water supplies. They have to jump off cliffs or scale down steep walls to the river...a river filled with hungry and huge crocodiles. It is a perilous journey. Some do not survive.

I have had an impression of this image in my head since I was a kid, maybe going back 60 years. It must have come to me from an old TV show like Mutual of Omaha's "Wild Kingdom," or a Disney special or a travel show like the early Lowell Thomas adventures. Somewhere it ended up as an image I could never forget. And then, in late 2018, there was the scene directly in front of me...and I had the good camera equipment and training to capture the shot. I focused on the beam of light and, when a wildebeest jumped through it, hit the button to capture the shot. It is exactly how I have pictured it in my head for all these years.

I have had only two such shots in my head...ever. The second one involved an elephant herd in a stand of trees at sunset. I got that shot later that afternoon. Strange...yup. I cannot explain how I came to have the images in my mind, or how they came to life for me...but they did.

If you would like to see the full images of both shots, go to my donhurzeler.com web page and they will be easy to find. They are available for purchase...and I know they look great because I have each one in my home printed on metal 40 inches by 60 inches. Just drop me a note at djhzz@aol.com and I will give you a quote on any size that might interest you.

The Back Cover Photo

In my last book, *What's Left of Don,* I told the story of getting in the water with salt water crocodiles to photograph them at Banco Chinchorro, Mexico. We had no protection...just us and the crocs. It was right out there at the limit of my nerves and I had to pretty much force myself to get in the water with them...but I did and I am glad I did.

At one point I had a large croc right in front of me...touching the dome of my camera housing with his nose from time to time. I stayed completely focused on him, even as a tropical storm pelted us with rain. You never want to take your eye off of a croc...they are sneaky and they are fast. We had been advised that crocodiles do not inflict injuries...if they get you, they tear you to shreds. So...that got my full attention.

However, as the storm stopped, I noticed a beautiful rainbow appear. I knew this was a unique opportunity, so I slowly moved to the side to get the rainbow to line up with the head of the croc...the croc being only about two feet in front of me at the time. I had already come up with the caption for the photo..."That story about the pot of gold at the end of the rainbow is a croc." I moved into position and got the shot.

I'll post the full photo on donhurzeler.com, along with a few other croc shots. I think you will find them horrifying...but it was quite an experience. They too are available for purchase.

Made in the USA
Las Vegas, NV
21 December 2020